THE RULE OF LA
MEASURE OF PR(

When property rights and environmental legislation clash, what
side should the Rule of Law weigh in on? It is from this point that
Jeremy Waldron explores the Rule of Law both from an historical
perspective – considering the property theory of John Locke – and
from the perspective of modern legal controversies. This critical
and direct account of the relation between the Rule of Law and the
protection of private property criticizes the view – associated with
the "World Bank model" of investor expectations – that a society
which fails to protect property rights against legislative restriction
is failing to support the Rule of Law. In this book, developed from
the 2011 Hamlyn Lectures, Waldron rejects the idea that the Rule of
Law privileges property rights over other forms of law, and argues
instead that the Rule of Law should endorse and applaud the use of
legislation to achieve valid social objectives.

JEREMY WALDRON is professor of law and philosophy at
the New York University School of Law, and Chichele Professor of
Social and Political Theory at All Souls College, Oxford University.
He has published extensively on the rule of law and property,
including *God, Locke and Equality* and *The Dignity of Legislation*.

THE RULE OF LAW
AND THE MEASURE
OF PROPERTY

JEREMY WALDRON

CAMBRIDGE
UNIVERSITY PRESS

555

CAMBRIDGE UNIVERSITY PRESS
Cambridge, New York, Melbourne, Madrid, Cape Town,
Singapore, São Paulo, Delhi, Mexico City

Cambridge University Press
The Edinburgh Building, Cambridge CB2 8RU, UK

Published in the United States of America by Cambridge University Press, New York

www.cambridge.org
Information on this title: www.cambridge.org/9781107653788

© Jeremy Waldron 2012

This publication is in copyright. Subject to statutory exception
and to the provisions of relevant collective licensing agreements,
no reproduction of any part may take place without the written
permission of Cambridge University Press.

First published 2012

Printed in the United Kingdom at the University Press, Cambridge

A catalogue record for this publication is available from the British Library

Library of Congress Cataloguing in Publication data
Waldron, Jeremy, author. The rule of law and the measure of property /
Jeremy Waldron.
   pages   cm. – (The Hamlyn lectures)
Includes bibliographical references and index.
ISBN 978-1-107-02446-5 (hardback) – ISBN 978-1-107-65378-8 (paperback)
1. Rule of law.   2. Property.   3. Right of property.   I. Title.
K3171.W33   2012
340'.11–dc23   2012016907

ISBN 978-1-107-02446-5 Hardback
ISBN 978-1-107-65378-8 Paperback

Cambridge University Press has no responsibility for the persistence or
accuracy of URLs for external or third-party internet websites referred to in
this publication, and does not guarantee that any content on such websites is,
or will remain, accurate or appropriate.

CONTENTS

v

PREFACE

I incurred many debts in the writing and delivery of the 2011 Hamlyn Lectures and in preparing them for publication. My greatest debts are to my audiences in Oxford, Coventry, and London, who listened patiently and responded with helpful and insightful questions. I am particularly grateful to Kim Economides for the initial invitation, Avrom Sherr for making many of the arrangements, and Finola O'Sullivan for being a patient editor at Cambridge University Press for such a dilatory author.

Timothy Endicott organized and chaired the first lecture at Oxford; Julio Faundez did the same at the University of Warwick for the second lecture, and Sir Stephen Sedley chaired the third lecture in London. New York University's D'Agostino Fund for Faculty Research helped support the rewriting of the lectures in Summer 2011. Carol Sanger helped me inestimably throughout the process, as always, with her support, insight, and love.

THE HAMLYN TRUST

The Hamlyn Trust owes its existence today to the will of the late Miss Emma Warburton Hamlyn of Torquay, who died in 1941 at the age of eighty. She came from an old and well-known Devon family. Her father, William Bussell Hamlyn, practiced in Torquay as a solicitor and Justice of the Peace for many years, and it seems likely that Miss Hamlyn founded the trust in his memory. Emma Hamlyn was a woman of strong character, intelligent, and cultured, well-versed in literature, music, and art, and a lover of her country. She traveled extensively in Europe and Egypt, and apparently took considerable interest in the law and ethnology of the countries and cultures that she visited. An account of Miss Hamlyn by Professor Chantal Stebbings of the University of Exeter may be found, under the title "The Hamlyn Legacy", in volume 42 of the published lectures.

Miss Hamlyn bequeathed the residue of her estate on trust in terms which it seems were her own. The wording was thought to be vague, and the will was taken to the Chancery Division of the High Court, which in November 1948 approved a Scheme for the administration of the trust. Paragraph 3 of the Scheme, which follows Miss Hamlyn's own wording, is as follows:

The object of the charity is the furtherance by lectures
or otherwise among the Common People of the United
Kingdom of Great Britain and Northern Ireland of
the knowledge of the Comparative Jurisprudence and
Ethnology of the Chief European countries including the
United Kingdom, and the circumstances of the growth
of such jurisprudence to the Intent that the Common
People of the United Kingdom may realise the privileges
which in law and custom they enjoy in comparison with
other European Peoples and realising and appreciating
such privileges may recognise the responsibilities and
obligations attaching to them.

The Trustees are to include the Vice-Chancellor of the
University of Exeter, representatives of the Universities of
London, Leeds, Glasgow, Belfast, and Wales and persons
co-opted. At present, there are eight Trustees:

Professor N. Burrows, University of Glasgow
Professor I. R. Davies, Swansea University
Ms Clare Dyer
Professor Chantal Stebbings (representing the Vice-Chancellor
    of the University of Exeter)
Professor R. Halson, University of Leeds
Professor J. Morison, Queen's University, Belfast
The Rt Hon. Lord Justice Sedley
Professor A. Sherr, Institute of Advanced Legal Studies,
    University of London (Chair)

From the outset, it was decided that the objects of the Trust
could be best achieved by means of an annual course of public lectures of outstanding interest and quality by eminent

lecturers, and by their subsequent publication and distribution to a wider audience. The first of the Lectures were delivered by the Rt Hon. Lord Justice Denning (as he then was) in 1949. Since then there has been an unbroken series of annual Lectures published until 2005 by Sweet & Maxwell and from 2006 by Cambridge University Press. A complete list of the Lectures may be found on the next page/overleaf. In 2005, the Trustees decided to supplement the Lectures with an annual Hamlyn Seminar, normally held at the Institute of Advanced Legal Studies in the University of London, to mark the publication of the Lectures in printed book form. The Trustees have also, from time to time, provided financial support for a variety of projects which, in various ways, have disseminated knowledge or have promoted to a wider public understanding of the law.

This, the 63rd series of lectures, was delivered by Professor Jeremy Waldron at the Gulbenkian Lecture Theatre at the University of Oxford, the Ramphal Lecture at the University of Warwick and in the Council Chamber at the Institute of Advanced Legal Studies. The Board of Trustees would like to record its appreciation to Professor Waldron and also the three university law schools, which generously hosted these Lectures.

AVROM SHERR
Institute of Advanced Legal Studies
Chairman of the Trustees
January 2011

THE HAMLYN LECTURES

1

The classical Lockean picture and its difficulties

These lectures are about private property and the Rule of Law. But, instead of starting with abstract definitions of these terms, I want to begin with a case.

It's a 1992 decision of the Supreme Court of the United States, *Lucas* v. *South Carolina Coastal Council*.[1] Like many American property cases, it concerns the application of what we call the "Takings Clause" of the Fifth Amendment. These lectures are not about American constitutional law and I won't ask you to venture very far into the morass that constitutes American Takings Clause jurisprudence. It is a mess and, if only you knew how much of a mess, you would thank me for steering us away from this aspect of litigation. But the facts in *Lucas* v. *South Carolina Coastal Council* are going to be very helpful for our discussion of ownership and its relation to the Rule of Law.[2]

In 1986, a property developer named David Lucas paid US$975,000 for some ocean-front real estate on the Isle of Palms, which is a barrier island off the coast of South

---

[1] 505 US 1003 (1992).

[2] My statement of the facts is taken from Justice Scalia's opinion for the Court in *Lucas* v. *South Carolina Coastal Council*, 505 US 1003 (1992), and also from the opinions given by judges in the South Carolina Supreme Court in *Lucas* v. *South Carolina Coastal Council*, 404 SE 2d 895 (1991).

Carolina, intending to develop it as residential property for resale. But his plans were thwarted by new environmental regulations established by state law intended to protect the coastline from erosion. Mr. Lucas knew at the time he bought the property that the general area was subject to some regulation under a 1972 federal statute and a 1977 statute of the South Carolina legislature. But his lots were not in what was defined as a "critical area" when he bought them, and so he did not need to apply for any special consent from the newly created South Carolina Coastal Council before beginning construction. However, things changed before he actually began construction. In 1988, responding to heightened concern about the state of the beaches expressed in the report of a blue-ribbon commission investigating the matter, South Carolina enacted legislation that empowered the Council to draw a new set-back line, a new line in the sand, as it were, a line that was on the landward side of Mr. Lucas's property. They did just that, and the effect was to establish a more or less complete ban on the construction of any habitable improvements on Mr. Lucas's land beyond a small deck or walkway.

So far as Mr. Lucas's plans for development were concerned, this rendered his property worthless. So he sued under the Fifth and Fourteenth Amendments of the US Constitution, which prohibit the taking of private property for public use without fair compensation. The case went all the way to the Supreme Court of the United States, and, in 1992, the Supreme Court held in Mr. Lucas's favor. The case was then remanded to the South Carolina courts which required South Carolina to pay Mr. Lucas US$850,000 for the two lots, just slightly less than he had bought them for. (I am told that now, twenty years later, large homes sit on both lots.)[3]

***

As I said, I do not intend to say very much more than this about the American Takings Clause. Suffice to say that the *Lucas* decision represented something of a revival of the Supreme Court's willingness to condemn state regulations as takings.[4] The questions I am going to consider are about a political ideal, not about constitutional provisions. The political ideal of the Rule of Law is something we valued in the United Kingdom, even though the UK has nothing like the Takings Clause in its constitution.[5] Even without anything like the American Fifth Amendment, prohibiting the taking of private property for public use without just compensation, we can still ask whether it detracts from the Rule of Law to subject property rights to restriction in the way regulations restricted the use Mr. Lucas could make of his property. For, suppose that a legal system generated a large number of

---

[3] See William A. Fischel, "A Photographic Update on Lucas v. South Carolina Coastal Council: A Photographic Essay," available at www.dartmouth.edu/~wfischel/lucasupdate.html.

[4] See e.g. Hope Babcock, "Has the US Supreme Court Finally Drained the Swamp of Takings Jurisprudence? The Impact of Lucas v. South Carolina Coastal Council on Wetlands and Coastal Barrier Beaches," *Harvard Environmental Law Review* 19 (1995), 1; and James Sanderson and Ann Mesmer, "A Review of Regulatory Takings after Lucas," *Denver University Law Review* 70 (1993), 497.

[5] The closest the UK gets to it is in Article 1 of the First Protocol to the European Convention on Human Rights, which is binding on the UK. But, as far as I understand, that provision has not been used much to constrain the regulation of property.

3

confrontations like this one – confrontations between private property rights on the one hand and environmental regulations on the other. Suppose that, up and down the coastline, and in inland wetland areas as well, and on mountains whose tops could be removed to find lucrative seams of coal, property owners found themselves limited in what they could do with their land by statutes and regulations, aimed at securing important public goods such as the preservation of beaches, an hospitable environment for birdlife, or the conservation of the aesthetic beauty of forests and mountains in an inland area. Such confrontations might be characterized in all sorts of ways. But here is the question that I want to ask: what is the situation regarding these property rights and environmental regulations so far as the Rule of Law is concerned? Does the Rule of Law condemn these restrictions? Does it require that the owner's lawful property rights be upheld? Or does it recognize the environmental regulations as law also, and command that they too should be respected, upheld and complied with as part of our general respect for the law of the land?

***

Let me get one distraction out of the way. In using *Lucas* as a sort of archetype, I am assuming for the sake of the argument I am going to pursue that the property-owner opposed and was offended by the restrictions on his property.[6] It is possible,

---

[6] According to Justice Scalia in *Lucas* v. *South Carolina Coastal Council*, 505 US 1003 (1992), p. 1009, "Lucas did not take issue with the validity of the Act as a lawful exercise of South Carolina's police power, but contended that the Act's complete extinguishment of his property's value entitled him to compensation regardless of whether the legislature had acted in furtherance of legitimate police power objectives."

though, that, in the *Lucas* litigation, the real estate developer didn't actually oppose the legislation. One way of understanding Mr. Lucas's complaint might be as follows:

> If my private property is to be affected by conservation schemes, then I am entitled to compensation. For if it is true that the public interest requires conservation of the beaches, then the costs of that conservation should be spread across the whole community; it should not be visited particularly on me.

That sounds like a reasonable claim. Mr. Lucas doesn't mean that he is having to pay for the bulldozing, the fencing, and the grass planting that is required to preserve the beaches. But he *is* having to bear the *opportunity cost* of having this land preserved as a beach – the opportunity cost of residential development, which the community is now insisting must be forgone. That's the cost that is unfairly incumbent on him, he will say, to the tune of almost a million wasted dollars. And what he is trying to do in his litigation against the Coastal Council is to secure a more equitable spread of costs across the community.

I have no quarrel with that argument (though others may). I mention it here, just to remove a distraction. Mr. Lucas may have been interested solely in compensation, but many people in a similar position do care about and do oppose the legislative restrictions as such. And some of them complain that such restrictions are at odds with the Rule of Law. *That* is the complaint I wish to discuss. Is it the role of the Rule of Law – considered as one of our most cherished political ideals – to protect people's property from these sorts of regulative incursions? Or should we reckon that the Rule of Law is as invested in the enforcement of environmental legislation as it is in the upholding of traditional property rights?

***

My question is about the Rule of Law, a phrase I always write using an upper-case "R" and an upper-case "L" to distinguish it from a phrase that sounds the same, but is all in lower case: "a rule of law," like the rule against perpetuities, the rule that prohibits drunk driving, or the rule that says I have to file my taxes in the United States by midnight on April 15. Those are all rules of law, but *the* Rule of Law is one of the great values or principles of our political system.

The idea of the Rule of Law is that the law should stand above every powerful person and agency in the land. The authority of government should be exercised within a constraining framework of public norms. Political power should be controlled by law – as the great Victorian relic, Albert Venn Dicey, put it, in contrast "with every system of government based on the exercise by persons in authority of wide, arbitrary, or discretionary powers."[7] Moreover, the Rule of Law requires that ordinary people should have access to law, in two senses. The first requires that law should be accessible, that is, promulgated prospectively as public knowledge so that people can take it on board and calculate its impact in advance on their actions and transactions. The second part of the Rule of Law's access requirement is that legal procedures should be

---

[7] A. V. Dicey, *Introduction to the Study of the Law of the Constitution* (8th edn, 1915) (Indianapolis, IN: Liberty Classics, 1982), p. 110 (emphasis added).

available to ordinary people to protect them against abuses of public and private power. All this in turn requires the independence of the judiciary, the accountability of government officials, the transparency of public business, and the integrity of legal procedures.

The Rule of Law is a hugely important ideal in our tradition and has been for millennia. It is sometimes said that Dicey in 1885 was the first jurist to use the phrase "the Rule of Law."[8] I don't think that is true, except in the most pedantic sense of exact grammatical construction. John Adams and other American revolutionaries explicitly contrasted the government of laws with the rule of men in 1780,[9] and Aristotle used almost exactly those terms (only in Greek) in Book III of the *Politics* more than 2,300 years ago.[10] I am not going to get hung up on the exact phraseology; the point is that, whether it is in the form of a slogan, a paragraph, or a treatise, and whether it's in English, Greek, or German, the ideals and concerns that this phrase connotes have resonated in our tradition for centuries – beginning with Aristotle, proceeding with medieval theorists like Sir John Fortescue, who sought to distinguish lawful from despotic forms of kingship, through the early modern period in the work of John Locke, James

[8] The claim that Dicey coined the phrase "the rule of law" has been traced to *Stephen's Commentaries on the Laws of England* (21st edn, London: Butterworths, 1895), vol. 3, p. 337.

[9] John Adams, who drafted the Constitution of Massachusetts, wrote in Article 30 of that document that the commonwealth aspired to be "a government of laws and not of men."

[10] Aristotle, *Politics*, trans. T. A. Sinclair (Harmondsworth: Penguin Books, 1962), pp. 122 ff. (Book III, Chapters 10 ff.).

Harrington, and (oddly enough) Niccolo Machiavelli, in the Enlightenment in the writings of Montesquieu, Beccaria, and others, in the American tradition in *The Federalist* and even more forcefully in *The Anti-Federalist Papers*, and, in the modern era, in Britain in the writings of Dicey, Hayek, Oakeshott, Raz, and Finnis, and in America in the writings of Fuller, Dworkin, and Rawls.[11]

There is a tremendous amount here, and quite a lot of detailed controversy about what the Rule of Law actually

[11] See Sir John Fortescue, *On the Laws and Governance of England*, ed. Shelley Lockwood (Cambridge: Cambridge University Press, 1997), pp. 85 ff.; John Locke, *Two Treatises of Government*, ed. Peter Laslett (Cambridge: Cambridge University Press, 1988); James Harrington, *The Commonwealth of Oceana and a System of Politics*, ed. J. G. A. Pocock (Cambridge: Cambridge University Press, 1992), pp. 9 ff.; Niccolò Machiavelli, *Discourses on Livy*, trans. Harvey Mansfield and Nathan Tarcov (Chicago: University of Chicago Press, 1996), pp. 73–76 and 93–95 (Book I, Chapters 34 and 45); Charles de Montesquieu, *The Spirit of the Laws*, ed. Anne Cohler, Basia Carolyn Miller, and Harold Samuel Stone (Cambridge: Cambridge University Press, 1989), pp. 156 ff. (Book II, Chapter 6); Cesare Beccaria, *On Crimes and Punishments and Other Writings*, ed. Richard Bellamy (Cambridge: Cambridge University Press, 1995); Alexander Hamilton, James Madison, and John Jay, *The Federalist Papers* (New York: Signet Classics, 2003), pp. 297–304 and 463–470 (Numbers 47 and 78); Ralph Ketcham (ed.), *The Anti-Federalist Papers* (New York: Signet Classics, 2003), pp. 256–308; Dicey, *Introduction to the Study of the Law of the Constitution*; F. A. Hayek, *The Constitution of Liberty* (Chicago: University of Chicago Press, 1960); Michael Oakeshott, "The Rule of Law" (1983), in *On History, and Other Essays* (Indianapolis, IN: Liberty Fund, 1999), p. 129; Joseph Raz, "The Rule of Law and Its Virtue," in his collection, *The Authority of Law* (Oxford: Clarendon Press, 1979), p. 224; John Finnis, *Natural Law and Natural Rights* (1980), pp. 270–276; Lon Fuller, *The Morality of Law* (New Haven, CT: Yale University Press, 1964); Ronald Dworkin, "Political Judges and the

requires, and what aspects of law it privileges.[12] Law is many things, after all: for some the Common Law is the epitome of legality; for others, the Rule of Law connotes the impartial application of a clearly drafted public statute; for others still, the Rule of Law is epitomized by a stable constitution that has been embedded for centuries in the politics of a country and the consciousness of its people. And people's estimation of the importance of the Rule of Law sometimes depends on which paradigm of law is being spoken about. When Aristotle contrasted the Rule of Law with the rule of men, he ventured the opinion that "a man may be a safer ruler than the written law, but not safer than the customary law."[13] Centuries later, in our own era, F. A. Hayek was at pains to distinguish the rule of law from the rule of legislation, identifying the former with something more like the evolutionary development of the Common Law, less constructive, less susceptible to human control, less *positivist* than the enactment of statutes.[14]

Plainly, these positions are going to be relevant to what we are considering in these lectures. Look at *Lucas v. South Carolina Coastal Council.* On the one hand, you have a property right developed presumably in accordance with the Common Law that South Carolina shares with many other

---

Rule of Law," in his collection, *A Matter of Principle* (Cambridge, MA: Harvard University Press, 1985), p. 9; and John Rawls, *A Theory of Justice* (Cambridge, MA: Harvard University Press, 1971), pp. 235–243.

[12] See Jeremy Waldron, "Is the Rule of Law an Essentially Contested Concept (in Florida)?," *Law and Philosophy* 21 (2002), 137.

[13] Aristotle, *Politics*, p. 144 (Book III, Chapter 16).

[14] F. A. Hayek, *Rules and Order*, vol. 1 of *Law, Legislation and Liberty* (Chicago: University of Chicago Press, 1973), pp. 72 ff.

jurisdictions – a property right defined by Common Law and circulating according to market principles. On the other hand, you have an environmental determination, made by an administrative body, pursuant to a piece of state legislation: a rule that exists as law because it occurred to some legislators in Columbia, South Carolina, that it might be a good idea to protect the beaches of the barrier islands from erosion. These are two different kinds of law – Common Law versus statutory regulation – and we may want to ask whether our ideal of the Rule of Law privileges one kind of law rather than the other. I am not going to try to settle any of this with an *a priori* definition. I want to leave it contestable, and I shall present everything I say in these lectures as a contribution to that contestation.

***

The fact that the Rule of Law is a controversial idea does not stop various agencies around the world from trying to measure it in different societies. The World Bank maintains a "Rule of Law" index for the nations of the earth, alongside other governance indicators such as control of corruption, absence of violence and so on. So for example, for 2008, a ranking was produced which placed countries like Canada, Norway, and New Zealand at the top of the Rule-of-Law League and Zimbabwe and Afghanistan at the bottom.[15] So here is another

---

[15] Daniel Kaufmann, Aart Kraay, and Massimo Mastruzzi, "Governance Matters VIII: Aggregate and Individual Governance Indicators, 1996–2008," available at http://ssrn.com/abstract=1424591. The organization, Political Risk Services, also produces Rule-of-Law assessments for every country which may be purchased from its website at http://www.prsgroup.com. See also the discussion of the work of Political Risk

way of asking our question. Should we expect a country's score on one of these Rule of Law indexes to go up or down depending on how much legislation there is of the kind that was at issue in *Lucas* v. *South Carolina Coastal Council*?

We might expect the indexes to be sensitive to this sort of thing, since they are supposed to be useful to businessmen who bring money to invest in enterprises in the subject country and want to know how far their investments will be affected or limited by social or environmental legislation. According to Harvard economics professor, Robert Barro:

> The general idea of these indexes is to gauge the attractiveness of a country's investment climate by considering the effectiveness of law enforcement, the sanctity of contracts, and the state of other influences on the security of property rights.[16]

Barro adds that "the willingness of customers to pay substantial amounts for this information is perhaps some testament to their validity."[17] But perhaps for this very reason we should be nervous about the integrity of these indexes, if they are skewed too much to the interests of outside investors. Not everyone supports the Rule of Law or cares about it; but is it really supposed to be biased in exactly this way? We normally think of the Rule of Law as something to be upheld in the interests of the subjects of the legal system in question,

Services in Robert Barro, "Democracy and the Rule of Law," in B. Bueno de Mesquita and H. Root (eds.), *Governing for Prosperity* (New Haven, CT: Yale University Press, 2000), p. 209, pp. 215 ff.
[16] Robert Barro, "Determinants of Democracy," *Journal of Political Economy* 107 (1999), S158, p. S173.
[17] *Ibid.*

in the interests of those who have to live with its demands, not as something to be upheld primarily in the interest of outsiders. Outsiders may be concerned about the Rule of Law in a given country, but that is an outside concern about how insiders are ruled, not an outside concern about how outsiders can profit.

***

The Rule of Law is one star in a constellation of ideals that dominate our political morality; others include democracy, human rights, and economic freedom. We want societies to be democratic; we want them to respect human rights; we want them to organize their economies around free markets and private property; and we want them to be governed in accordance with the Rule of Law. But constellations can deceive us. The juxtaposition of stars in a constellation is not necessarily indicative of their actual proximity to one another. Their apparent proximity may be just an artifact of where they present themselves in our visual field – the sky, as we call it – which for us is basically two-dimensional even though in astronomical fact it reaches in a third dimension away from us almost to infinity.[18]

So too in the constellation of our ideals. We think of democracy and the Rule of Law or human rights and the Rule of Law as close, even overlapping ideals. But it may be

---

[18] Stars may appear close enough to one another to be grouped into a single formation – the Southern Cross or whatever – yet that is just the way they seem. The apparent proximity of (say) Mimosa and Gacrux in the Southern Cross formation – the giant blue star at the left hand beam and the cool red giant at the top of the cross – belies the fact that the latter (a cool red giant) is much closer to earth than the former (88 light years as opposed to 353 light years away).

important to maintain a sense of the distance between them. There are multiple ways in which we evaluate social and political systems, multiple ways in which social and political structures may respond to or excite our concerns, and unless we buy into a very general holism – something like the position put forward in Ronald Dworkin's new book, *Justice for Hedgehogs*, in which all our ideals, however scattered, come down more or less to the self-same thing[19] – there is not a lot to be gained by collapsing any one of them into any of the others.

This is a point we owe to a very influential article by Joseph Raz, published many years ago, where Raz insisted on analytic grounds that "the Rule of Law" should not be regarded as the name of all good things:

> [T]he rule of law is just one of the virtues which a legal system may possess and by which it is to be judged …
> A non-democratic legal system, based on the denial of human rights, on extensive poverty, on racial segregation, sexual inequalities, and religious persecution may, in principle, conform to the requirements of the rule of law better than any of the legal systems of the more enlightened Western democracies. This does not mean that it will be better than those Western democracies. It will be an immeasurably worse legal system, but it will excel in one respect: in its conformity to the rule of law.[20]

This indicates a sort of separation thesis between the Rule of Law and our other political values like human rights or

---

[19] See Ronald Dworkin, *Justice for Hedgehogs* (Cambridge, MA: Harvard University Press, 2010), pp. 1–2.

[20] Raz, "The Rule of Law and Its Virtue," p. 211.

democracy. Interrogating it and upholding Raz's thesis will be the point of much that follows in this book.

Of course, even if we adopt Raz's separation thesis, we must expect to come across some overlaps. For example, although a society may respect the Rule of Law while scoring low in its human rights record, it cannot ignore *all* human rights, because some rights require exactly what the Rule of Law requires. Articles 7 through 11 of the Universal Declaration of Human Rights are a case in point, with their prohibitions on arbitrary arrest and retroactive law and their requirements of equality before the law and the entitlement of each person "to a fair and public hearing by an independent and impartial tribunal, in the determination of ... any criminal charge against him." It does not follow that the Rule of Law and human rights amount to the same thing; what it means is that codes of human rights are one of the ways in which we uphold some of the most important requirements of the Rule of Law.

Our inquiry is about the relation between the Rule of Law and one other star in the constellation – our ideal of economic freedom and, by implication, private property. Are these distinct ideals – relatively distant from one another in the constellation – capturing quite different concerns about the way we run our society? Or are they more closely related than that? Do they do work for one another – as we saw human rights doing some work for the Rule of Law – so that the Rule of Law for example is one of the ways in which we protect economic freedom? Or *vice versa*: does respect for property promote the Rule of Law? A suggestion to that effect was made by Alexis de Tocqueville, who argued that the wide distribution of property rights helped sustain a fondness for law and an awareness of its importance among Americans at the beginning of the nineteenth century.[21] There were suggestions of a similar kind in the twentieth century as well. In 1991, James W. Ely gave a book that he had written about the constitutional protection of property the title *The Guardian of Every Other Right*, attributing this characterization to Arthur Lee of Virginia in a pamphlet published in 1775.[22]

Even if the separation thesis is true, we know that traditional conceptions of the Rule of Law emphasize legal constancy as something to be valued, and presumably private property rights, being legal rights, are to have the benefit of the same constancy or stability (argued for under the auspices of the Rule of Law) as any other legal rights. And this is not an inconsiderable point. (I will explore the relation between property and ordinary legal security in much more detail in Chapter 2.) Also, predictability is often cited as a Rule-of-Law virtue. Though, in his well-known recent book on the subject, Lord Bingham gave little or no privilege to property as such, he did insist as a very first principle that "[t]he law must be ... so far as possible intelligible, clear and predictable."[23] And he indicated that one of the most important things people needed from the law that governed them was predictability in the conduct of their lives and businesses. Bingham quoted Lord Mansfield to the effect that "[i]n all mercantile transactions the great object should be certainty ... [I]t is of more consequence

[21] Alexis de Tocqueville, *Democracy in America* (New York: Alfred A. Knopf, 1994), pp. 244–248 (vol. I, Chapter 14). See also the discussion in the text accompanying Chapter 3, note 32, below.
[22] James W. Ely, *The Guardian of Every Other Right: A Constitutional History of Property Rights* (New York: Oxford University Press, 1997), p. 18.
[23] T. Bingham, *The Rule of Law* (Harmondsworth: Allen Lane, 2010), p. 37.

that a rule should be certain, than whether the rule is established one way rather than the other."[24] Bingham went on to observe in his own voice that "[n]o one would choose to do business … involving large sums of money, in a country where parties' rights and obligations were undecided."[25] So all that might redound as a general matter to the benefit of property rights, even if the separation thesis is correct.

Perhaps we should not go very far beyond that. In defense of the separation thesis, we might cite the many canonical figures in the Rule-of-Law literature who seem to have had no interest in making any explicit connection between property and the Rule of Law. Aristotle, who wrote extensively about both topics, said nothing about any connection.[26] Nor did Dicey make any connection with property except obliquely in a reference to "goods" in his first principle of the Rule of Law: "[N]o man is punishable or can be lawfully made to suffer in body *or goods* except for a distinct breach of law established in the ordinary legal manner before the ordinary Courts of the land."[27] Nor did Lon Fuller.[28] Nor did Joseph

---

[24] Lord Mansfield in *Vallejo v. Wheeler* (1774) 1 Cowp 143, p. 153 (cited by Bingham, *The Rule of Law*, p. 38).

[25] Bingham, *The Rule of Law*, p. 38.

[26] In Aristotle's *Politics*, there is a fine discussion of property at pp. 62 ff. (Book II, Chapters 5–6) and there is a seminal discussion of the Rule of Law at pp. 121 ff. (Book III, Chapters 10–11). But Aristotle does not connect the two.

[27] Dicey, *Introduction to the Study of the Law of the Constitution*, p. 110 (emphasis added).

[28] In Fuller, *The Morality of Law*, pp. 59–61 and 75–76, there is some discussion of the relation between the "inner morality of law" and taxation. But it is simply an exploration of the possibility that tax laws

Raz.[29] And, apart from the passages I cited a moment ago, Tom Bingham said next to nothing about a connection between property and the Rule of Law except in a brief passage on the implications of Article 1 of the First Protocol to the European Convention on Human Rights.[30]

On the other hand, an association between the Rule of Law and the principle of private property is not unfamiliar or preposterous as would be, for example, a suggestion that the Rule of Law required government support for the performing arts or a more powerful and effective military. It is certainly familiar in the vernacular use that is made of the Rule-of-Law ideal, just maybe not in the narrowly focused philosophic literature. So it is worth entertaining. I think it is incumbent on us to explore the implications of the vernacular use of the Rule of Law. For this ideal is not the property of the analytic philosophers and it is certainly not our job as jurisprudes to go

may sometimes infringe on Fuller's principle of prospectivity and practicability. There is no discussion of the relation between the Rule of Law and property.

[29] The closest that Raz comes to connecting the Rule of Law and property in his essay, "The Rule of law and its Virtue," is at pp. 226–229, in his brief critique of Hayek's perspective.

[30] Lord Bingham, in *The Rule of Law*, pp. 82–83, said he thought that the First Protocol (Article 1) of the European Convention on Human Rights "prohibits the arbitrary confiscation of people's property ... without compensation." He added that "[t]he treatment of white farmers in Zimbabwe would be the most obvious violation." But Bingham also indicated the importance of acknowledging the necessity in some circumstances of overriding property rights for the benefit of the community as a whole: "It may be necessary to control the way I use my land to prevent my factory polluting the atmosphere or the local river ... But all this must be done pursuant to law, as the rule of law requires."

round reproaching laymen for not using the idea in the way that (for example) Joseph Raz uses it.

I mentioned Aristotle, Dicey, Fuller, Raz, and Tom Bingham as Rule-of-Law thinkers who have not pursued this connection with property. But there *are* other philosophers who have insisted – and insisted quite emphatically – on the connection that interests us. The latter part of this chapter will be devoted to John Locke, whose account is one of the most extensive. But, closer to our modern interests, we should also mention Friedrich Hayek, whose work since *The Road to Serfdom* has concentrated on the special threat that socialist administration and appeals to social justice pose to the Rule of Law – and that argument seems to implicate private property, at least indirectly.[31] And others have said something similar. Ronald Cass of Boston University says that "[a] critical aspect of the commitment to the rule of law is the definition and protection of property rights."

> [T]he degree to which the society is bound by law, is committed to processes that allow property rights to be secure under legal rules that will be applied predictably and not subject to the whims of particular individuals, matters. The commitment to such processes is the essence of the rule of law.[32]

Finally, we should not forget Richard Epstein, who has written extensively on these matters, and whose work has moved from

[31] See e.g. F. A. Hayek, *The Road to Serfdom* (London: George Routledge, 1944), and *The Fatal Conceit: The Errors of Socialism* (Chicago: University of Chicago Press, 1991).
[32] Ronald A. Cass, "Property Rights Systems and the Rule of Law," Boston University School of Law Working Paper Series, Public Law and Legal Theory No. 03-06, available at http://ssrn.com/abstract=392783.

pursuing the Rule of Law and the ideal of a free, private prop-
erty-based economy as parallel pillars of a free society – com-
plementing one another, and perhaps (as they used to say in
working class areas) taking in one another's washing, without
necessarily merging into a single ideal – to a more aggressive
account in his most recent writing suggesting that an analytic
separation of the two ideals may leave the Rule of Law impov-
erished, oddly isolated from the reality of our formal and procedural concerns about contemporary public administration.[33]
The case Epstein makes is a powerful one and it deserves our
consideration – all the more so because Epstein actually concedes at the outset the conceptual point that "[a]nalytically, the
rule of law is … a separate conception from private property
and personal liberty."[34] He concedes this, but still he provides
some good reasons for thinking that such analytical strictures
should not be the end of the matter. Epstein says that "a close
connection" between the Rule of Law and private property "can
… be established empirically by showing … that the cumula-
tive demands of the modern social democratic state require a
range of administrative compromises and shortcuts that will

[33] Compare Richard Epstein, "Property Rights and the Rule of Law:
Classical Liberalism Confronts the Modern Administrative State"
(unpublished), available at www.law.nyu.edu/ecm_dlv2/groups/public/@
nyu_law_website__academics__colloquia__legal_political_and_social_
philosophy/documents/documents/ecm_pro_062726.pdf with Richard
Epstein, *Design for Liberty: Private Property, Public Administration, and
the Rule of Law* (Cambridge, MA: Harvard University Press, 2011), p. 10.
I am grateful to Professor Epstein for having made the manuscript of the
latter work available to me in advance of publication, during the drafting
of my Hamlyn Lectures.
[34] Epstein, *Design for Liberty*, p. 10.

eventually gut the rule of law in practice, even if it honors it in theory."[35] A lot of what I am doing in this book can be read as a response to Professor Epstein's extraordinarily rich, provocative, and influential ideas.

What Epstein suggests are two strategies for developing a link between the Rule of Law and private property. The connection can be pursued negatively, under the auspices of a more general Rule-of-Law attack on the kind of unstable, inconstant and often frankly discretionary regulation that threatens property as a matter of fact, and the sort of public administration that usually goes along with it. Or it can be pursued more affirmatively in terms of a special and explicit connection between private property and the Rule of Law so that private property is one of the things that the Rule of Law aims to promote just as it aims to promote prospectivity or natural justice.

Most of what I will be saying in the book is about the second, affirmative strategy. But Epstein's negative strategy is an interesting one too. Since Dicey, the Rule of Law has been associated with a critique of discretionary administration, and since, on many views, it is discretionary administration that poses the greatest threat to private property, it may be that enforcing this general doctrine of legality in governance is all one needs to do in order to protect property.[36] It is a little bit like Lon Fuller's famous argument that, if we rigorously follow the formal principles he calls the internal morality of law, we will find it much harder to violate external

---

[35] *Ibid.*, p. 12.
[36] Dicey, *Introduction to the Study of the Law of the Constitution*, pp. lv–lxi.

or substantive morality.[37] Fuller thought it was no accident that the Nazis, for example, found it necessary to violate all sorts of formal principles of legality in order to pursue their racist and murderous aims; and analogously it may be thought to be no accident that those who assault private property rights tend to use methods of governance at odds with the formal and procedural principles of the Rule of Law. The second, more affirmative strategy is to develop and justify a substantive conception of the Rule of Law that explicitly embraces the principle of private property. In the end, I am skeptical about that, but it cannot be ruled out, at least not out of hand. So I will give it a run for its money in Chapter 2.

***

However, I first want to consider a slightly different move. Some commentators draw a distinction between the Rule of Law and what they call rule *by* law.[38] They celebrate the one and disparage the other. The one is supposed to lift law above politics. The other – rule by law – indicates the instrumental use of law (legal forms and legal procedures) as a tool of political power.

---

[37] See Lon Fuller, "Positivism and Fidelity to Law: A Reply to Hart," *Harvard Law Review* 71 (1959), 630, pp. 636–637, 644–646, and 648–657.

[38] For examples of the use of this distinction, see Brian Tamanaha, *On the Rule of Law: History, Politics, Theory* (Cambridge: Cambridge University Press, 2004), p. 3. See also Jeffrey Kahn, "The Search for the Rule of Law in Russia," *Georgetown Journal of International Law* 37 (2006), 353, p. 368; Charles Lugosi, "Rule of Law or Rule by Law? The Detention of Yaser Hamdi," *American Journal of Criminal Law* 30 (2003), 225, pp. 266 ff.; David Dyzenhaus, "Schmitt v. Dicey: Are States of Emergency Inside or Outside the Legal Order," *Cardozo Law Review* 27 (2006), 2005, pp. 2018 ff.

So let me go a little deeper into this distinction, because those who make it think it is very important.

The theorists I have in mind are willing to concede that the administrative enforcement of a duly enacted environmental statute in the *Lucas* case represents rule by law. The environmentalists are politically in the ascendant in South Carolina. But, instead of just dictatorially *imposing* their preference for beach conservation on the barrier islands, they have had the decency to at least go to the trouble of getting the legislature in Columbia to enact legislation, and they have proceeded rigorously to make regulations in the proper form under the powers conferred in that statute. That is rule by law – rule by these men and women in South Carolina using law for their own purposes – and it is certainly better than a Mugabe-style invasion of property that has no legal credentials at all.

Still, rule by law – say these commentators – is not the same as the Rule *of* Law, where in fact law itself governs a situation or is supposed to govern a situation, without the help of people – environmentalists, power-hungry legislators, or anyone else. You may ask: how is that supposed to happen? After all, all law is made by people and interpreted by people and applied by people. It can no more rule us by itself, without human assistance, than (in Harrington's image, attributed to Hobbes) a cannon can dominate us without an iron-monger to cast it and an artilleryman to load and fire it.[39]

---

[39] Harrington, *The Commonwealth of Oceana*, p. 9, referring to Thomas Hobbes, *Leviathan*, ed. Richard Tuck (Cambridge: Cambridge University Press, 1996), p. 471.

The theorists I am discussing may acknowledge the ontological point. But, undeterred, they say there is nevertheless a real sense in which the operation of a system of private property represents law itself governing a situation. Nobody in authority had to decide that David Lucas should be in charge of these residential lots on Beachwood East in the Isle of Palms. That property circulated into his hands as a result of a series of individual transactions in which the rulers, the authorities, played no part. The market transactions that led up to his becoming the owner of this real estate took place under the auspices and within the framework of the law of property, which is part of the Common Law of South Carolina. In South Carolina as elsewhere, the Common Law is not the product of any legislative decision; it is something that has evolved in a largely unintended way through a series of interconnecting judgments. Legal positions *emerge* rather than being dictated by legislative *fiat*. What's important here is an image of the autonomous operation of the Common Law. It is the ascendancy of Common Law that enables us to say that law rules rather than any politician rules in regard to property rights. By contrast, it seems impossible to deny that the ascendancy of environmental legislation *represents* the rule of men, albeit men ruling by statutory means. Human politicians in the South Carolina legislature chose to make this law and the law in question is exactly the law they opted to impose.

In making this contrast, I don't mean that Common Law property rights are unrestricted. They may or may not be. But, even if they are not unrestricted, many of the restrictions in an autonomous property system are themselves the result of emergent, rather than imposed, Common Law doctrines. The

23

restrictions emerge without any official *fiat* either in the form of restrictive covenants or in terms of private law principles of nuisance. Once again, their emergence or their application to any particular piece of real estate is not the result of any ruler's decision.

Another way of grasping this distinction between the Rule of Law and rule by law relies on a differentiation between the way private law operates and the way public law operates. As far as I can tell, the theorists who use the distinction between Rule of Law and rule by law want to associate the former more or less exclusively with private law. They endorse the doctrine propounded by Montesquieu in *The Spirit of the Laws* that we should keep private law and public law apart and "[t]hat we should not regulate by the Principles of political Law those Things which depend on the Principles of civil Law."[40] "Civil law" – Montesquieu's word for what we are calling private law – is, he said, "the Palladium of property," and it should be allowed to operate according to its own logic, not burdened with the principles of public or political regulation.

So there you have it. Environmental regulation is the work of human hands – it is a gift of the state to the beaches,

---

[40] Montesquieu, *The Spirit of the Laws*, p. 511 (Book 26, Chapter 15). Equally, Montesquieu says we shouldn't decide public matters by civil law analogies, e.g. succession by inheritance etc. "The order of succession is not fixed for the sake of the reigning family; but because it is the interest of the state that it should have a reigning family. The law which regulates the succession of individuals is a civil law, whose view is the interest of individuals; that which regulates the succession to monarchy is a political law, which has in view the welfare and preservation of the kingdom." *Ibid.*, p. 512.

the mountaintops, or the birds who revel in the wetland habitat – but property rights are not. Property rights come from the bottom up. And this is a theme that Richard Epstein also insists upon. Property rights are not a gift of the state, he says; they have legal standing quite apart from human rule. "No system of property rights," says Epstein, "rests on the premise that the state may bestow or deny rights in things to private persons on whatever terms it sees fit." Rather, he says, "the correct starting point is the Lockean position that property rights come from the bottom up."[41] And, on Epstein's account, it is precisely misapprehensions about this point that have brought us to the courtroom in cases like *Lucas* v. *South Carolina Coastal Council*, "invert[ing] the relationship between individual rights and political power."

> The classical liberal theory sees limited government as a means to defend the fundamental rights of property …
> The modern democratic state, by contrast, defines itself in opposition to any theory of natural law that posits these individual "pre-political" entitlements as existing prior to the creation of the state. Instead, property rights are arbitrary assemblages of rights that the state creates for its own instrumental purposes, and which it can undo almost at will for the same instrumental ends.[42]

To see the proper relation, then, between the Rule of Law and private ownership, we have to be prepared to turn the tables on the modern administrative state and go back to something like a Lockean account of the constraining force of property. That is Richard Epstein's position.

[41] Epstein, *Design for Liberty*, p. 99.
[42] *Ibid.*, p. 63.

25

We might as well confront this position head-on. And for this reason I have titled my first chapter: "The Classical Lockean Picture and Its Difficulties." John Locke and his works have been very much my obsession since my doctoral work on property at Oxford in the 1970s and 1980s. I have written extensively on Locke's theory of property and on his political philosophy more generally.[43] The discussion in this chapter gives me an opportunity to bring my interest in John Locke into closer relation with my more recent interest in the Rule of Law.

***

Locke, as you know, explained property as a natural right.[44] He saw property rights as rights that could be generated and sustained by labor and exchange, and recognized as such in a human community without benefit of any edicts of positive law. In Locke's system, property was generated by the unilateral action of appropriators and cultivators approaching unowned resources without any authorization. The rights arise out of what they decide, on their own motion, to do. They are

---

[43] Jeremy Waldron, "Locke's Account of Inheritance and Bequest," *Journal of the History of Philosophy* 19 (1981), 39; "The Turfs My Servant Has Cut," *The Locke Newsletter* 13 (1982), 9; "Two Worries About Mixing One's Labour," *Philosophical Quarterly* 33 (1983), 37; "Locke, Tully and the Regulation of Property," *Political Studies* 32 (1984), 98; *The Right to Private Property* (Oxford: Oxford University Press, 1988), Chapter 5; "Nozick and Locke: Filling the Space of Rights," *Social Philosophy and Policy* 22 (2005), 81; *God, Locke, and Equality: Christian Foundations of Locke's Political Thought* (Cambridge: Cambridge University Press, 2002), Chapter 6.

[44] Locke, *Two Treatises of Government*, pp. 285–302 (Book II, Chapter 5, §§ 25–51).

generated, as Epstein puts it, from the bottom up. And all that people need from positive law, when they set up a legal system to overcome certain difficulties in the state of nature, are principles of private law to recognize and accommodate the existence of property rights that are already well-established and facilitate their circulation.[45] "The reason why men enter into society," says Locke, "is the preservation of their Property," and that, as he said, presupposes that people already have property and that property is neither the work nor the plaything of public law.[46]

Well, I am a follower of John Locke in many things, but I am not convinced. I am here in quest of an open-eyed clear-headed view of these matters – of the relation between the Rule of Law and private property – and I do not find that in Locke's account, nor do I find it in the work of twentieth-century political philosophers like Robert Nozick, who built upon Locke's theory.[47] In this last part of the chapter, I want to develop two lines of critical thought about the Lockean project and its relation to the issue we are considering. First, I want to consider whether we can possibly accord any credence to Locke on what Epstein calls the "bottom-up" private law origins of the property rights that interest us. And, secondly, I want to consider the tensions in Locke's political and constitutional theory that arise from the juxtaposition of formal and substantive elements in his conception the Rule of Law.

---

[45] *Ibid.*, p. 412 (Book II, Chapter 19, § 222).
[46] *Ibid.*, p. 360 (Book II, Chapter 11, § 138).
[47] Robert Nozick, *Anarchy, State and Utopia* (Oxford: Basil Blackwell, 1974), Chapter 7.

Let me begin with the basic credibility of the Lockean account. Many years ago, I was asked to give a talk to a conference of Federated Farmers in New Zealand on Locke and Nozick and their view of private property.[48] The farmers, politically very influential in New Zealand, were facing a number of irksome environmental statutes and they wanted some philosophical vindication of their rights in their land as Lockean natural entitlements to set up against these legislative incursions. I told them I didn't think it was possible. Nothing like the Lockean account is plausible, historically, as an account of the origin of current rights over land in New Zealand. Locke's theory has it that property rights in their origin are independent of government and law. But consider the history – the chain of title – of a typical New Zealand farm. I am going to give you an imaginary history, constructed for this lecture. But it is not, I think, atypical.

> In 2011, a farmer – we will call him John Gardner – is
> in possession of a piece of land and very annoyed about
> environmental restrictions on the use that he can make of
> it. But how did it come to be his? Well, we may suppose that
> Gardner has farmed this land for many years. He purchased
> it in 1992 from a public trustee, a Mr. Dworkin, who took
> it over when the previous farmer, name of Hart, went into
> bankruptcy in 1985. Hart had inherited the farm from his
> father, Goodhart, when the latter died intestate in 1972.
> Goodhart in turn had purchased it in 1930 for a song from
> a company that had held it in trust after it had been farmed

[48] "Property Rights from Magna Carta to the Twenty-First Century," Address to New Zealand Federated Farmers by Satellite Link: San Francisco to Wellington, July 1996.

for a couple of generations by the Austin family. Records reveal that Austin bought the land in an auction sponsored by the Bank of New Zealand (which in those days was a wholly government-owned enterprise), the bank having foreclosed on a feckless settler called Bentham in 1890. At an earlier stage, Bentham purchased the land at a bargain price from a man called Blackstone in the 1880s who had held, first the leasehold, and then the freehold, from the colonial government since 1865. The colonial government, in turn, had bought it from a Maori tribe in whose collective possession it had been for some centuries, since the (relatively recent) commencement of human habitation in New Zealand about 800 years ago.

Now many things can be said about this story, besides the fact that it is imaginary but typical. One thing you cannot say is that property rights in Gardner's farm originated in the labor of a Lockean individual before the institution of government or civil society. There are fragments or strings of historical entitlement here and there, with the land passing by consensual transactions of sale, purchase, and inheritance between individuals. But mostly the land seems to have been governed by social and public legal arrangements from start to finish. It was used and cultivated first by a collective group, its original Maori owners, with ownership and administration at the tribal and hence the political level rather than the individual level. It was then transferred by the indigenous tribe – whether by respectable or dubious transactions is something New Zealand tribunals are currently trying to assess[49] – to

[49] See the description of the Waitangi Tribunal at www.waitangi-tribunal.govt.nz.

the colonial government as part of that government's right of pre-emption (established under the Treaty of Waitangi).[50] The British government's policy of encouraging white settlement led them to offer the leasehold in this land to enterprising settlers. And their policy of encouraging family farming in New Zealand led them to redistribute some of the leaseholds and then convert leasehold to freehold property. The transition from indigenous tribal property to government property to leasehold property on the government's terms to individual freehold is something that was supervised by the state purportedly in the public interest at every stage. And at every stage modifications to the conveyancing laws, in farmers' ability to alienate government leaseholds, in the laws of trusts and bankruptcy, and in the laws of inheritance, family provision, and intestacy – these modifications all took place not through some inexorable logic endogenous to private law (let alone natural law), but by statute (mainly) and (occasionally) by judge-made law – in both cases, law-making oriented explicitly to the policy needs of New Zealand as an economy

---

[50] Treaty of Waitangi 1840, Article 2: "Her Majesty the Queen of England confirms and guarantees to the Chiefs and Tribes of New Zealand … the full exclusive and undisturbed possession of their Lands and Estates Forests Fisheries and other properties which they may collectively or individually possess so long as it is their wish and desire to retain the same in their possession; but the Chiefs of the United Tribes and the individual Chiefs yield to Her Majesty the exclusive right of Pre-emption over such lands as the proprietors thereof may be disposed to alienate at such prices as may be agreed upon between the respective Proprietors and persons appointed by Her Majesty to treat with them in that behalf."

and to what was for a long time a public commitment to the diffusion of property rights and broad economic equality.[51]

So, if farmer Gardner were to oppose the imposition of some environmental statute affecting his farm on the ground that this was a public law interference with private law rights that historically had never been at the mercy of government in this way, or if he wanted to oppose the legislation on the normative ground of the Lockean basis of his property rights, we would have to say that his claim was fatuous. There might be many things to be said for or against the environmental legislation that worried him; but the property right impacted by the legislation would seem to have been throughout its entire history as much an artifact of public law as the environmental statute itself. If the property right is to be set up against the environmental legislation, it is as one artifact of public law versus another, not (as Epstein suggests) as an entirely different sort of right whose posture in this conflict is a matter of the rule of private law and has nothing to do with the legislative rule by men.

The New Zealand case is easy owing to the very prominent role of public authorities in regard to native ownership, in regard to late-nineteenth-century land reform, in regard to the distribution of modern property rights, and the continuing role of institutions like the Public Trustee. But I suspect that a similar tale can be told in most legal systems, with variations

[51] See the discussion of the Lands for Settlement Acts 1892, 1894, and 1908 in Tom Brooking, *Lands for the People? A Biography of John McKenzie* (Dunedin: Otago University Press, 1995); and James Belich, *Paradise Reforged: A History of the New Zealanders* (London: Allen Lane, 2001), pp. 128 ff.

no doubt, but in ways that equally undermine the myth that modern property rights can trace their standing to anything remotely like a Lockean provenance.

And all this is without even considering the respectability or integrity of the various links in the allegedly Lockean chain. In Locke's story, particularly in Robert Nozick's version of Locke's story, the importance of respecting a current property right presupposes that it is the culmination of an unbroken series of consensual transactions stretching back to the dawn of time.[52] The entitlement is historically based, and of course this means that its legitimacy is at the mercy of history. But what if, when you delve back through the archives, you find a fraudulent transaction in the early twentieth century or an instance of outright theft or expropriation in the nineteenth? Then, by the logic of the Lockean approach, the current land is stolen property; it is as though you bought a car from a man who bought it from a man who stole it from its owner. The defect in the title infects every subsequent step.[53] Or if it does not – if we apply some doctrine of positive law that allows historical defects to be washed out by the passage of time or by certain forms of uncontested registration of title – then once again we must give up any sense that the property right emerges from the nightmare of fraud and injustice blinking in the sunlight of the twenty-first century as something pure that evolved bottom-up in the realm of private law. No: it emerges now as an artifact of the interaction of public law and private law – a sort of fugue-like relation between them – and

---

[52] Nozick, *Anarchy, State and Utopia*, pp. 150 ff.
[53] *Ibid.*, pp. 152–153.

once again there seems no reason why other forms of inter-action such as environmental regulation or restrictions on use should not also be orchestrated in this way. By the way, I think Robert Nozick recognized this. He articulated the structure of Lockean historical entitlement, not because he believed that such a theory vindicated contemporary property holdings in the United States but because he wanted to understand what justice in these matters would be like, in the unlikely event it existed. Nozick was too honorable a man to be of much use to the triumphant Right in the 1980s and 1990s. He was never prepared to say that a Lockean theory legitimized contem-porary disparities of wealth in the United States. On the con-trary, he thought it undeniable that contemporary holdings in America would be condemned as unjust by any remotely plausible conception of historical entitlement.[54]

People are made very uncomfortable about all this. Certainly, my audience at Federated Farmers was. As William Blackstone put it in his *Commentaries on the Laws of England*, we all get very intoxicated with the idea of property – *our* property – but yet

> we seem afraid to look back to the means by which it was acquired, as if fearful of some defect in our title; or at best we rest satisfied with the decision of the laws in our favour, without examining the reason or authority upon which those laws have been built.[55]

[54] *Ibid.*, pp. 230–231. See also Jeremy Waldron, "Nozick and Locke: Filling the Space of Rights," *Social Philosophy and Policy* 22 (2005), 81, pp. 103–104.
[55] William Blackstone, *Commentaries on the Laws of England*, ed. Wayne Morrison (London: Cavendish Publishing, 2001), vol. II, Chapter 1, p. 3.

Still, that is what I think we have to do, in order to get a clear-headed and honest sense of the relation between private property and the Rule of Law.

Locke's account fails. We cannot use a distinction between private law and public law, or a distinction between the Rule of Law and rule by law to vindicate any claim that property rights are privileged over public legislation in the sort of stand-off we are considering. There is no getting away from the fact that property rights are entangled in public legislation. Or, to put it in a form that bears directly on the case we are considering, legislation like South Carolina's Beachfront Management Act is unlikely to have been the first public law intervention in regard to the definition and redefinition of the property rights held by Mr. Lucas and his predecessors in title.

***

Many critics will want to leave the matter there. But I would like to hammer one more nail into the Lockean coffin. John Locke is one of our earliest theorists of the Rule of Law, in the account he gives in Chapter 7 of the *Second Treatise* on the importance of equality before the law and the repudiation of absolutism, in the account he gives in Chapter 12 of the relation between the Rule of Law and the separation of powers, and above all in his extensive discussion in Chapter 11 of the formal limits that he wants to impose upon legislatures.

It is the last of these that I want to focus on. In Locke's discussion of the Rule of Law, what he emphasizes is the importance of governance through "established standing Laws, promulgated and known to the People." Locke uses these Rule-of-Law phrases over and over again: "established standing Laws," "declared and received Laws," "settled, known

Law, received and allowed by common consent [throughout the community] to be the Standard of Right and Wrong."[56] The contrast is with rule by "extemporary Arbitrary Decrees" or "undetermined Resolutions." "The Legislative, or Supream Authority," we are told, "cannot assume to its self a power to Rule by extemporary Arbitrary Decrees." It must rule through "established standing Laws, promulgated and [made] known to the People."[57]

Now, the term "arbitrary," which Locke uses over and over again, is a weasel word. It means many different things. Sometimes it means "oppressive." But, when Locke is distinguishing the rule of settled standing laws from arbitrary decrees, it is not the oppressive sense of "arbitrary" that he has in mind. In this context, something is arbitrary because it is extemporary: there is no notice of it; the ruler just figures it out as he goes along. It is the arbitrariness of unpredictability, not knowing what you can rely on, being subject, as Locke put it, to someone's "sudden thoughts, or unrestrain'd, and till that moment unknown Wills without having any measures set down which may guide and justifie their actions."[58] And so it is an arbitrariness that might be associated not just with an oppressive ruler, but even with one who is trying as hard as he can to figure out and apply the law of nature on a retail basis.

You see, in Locke's story, one of the things that people wanted to get away from in state of nature was being subject

---

[56] Locke, *Two Treatises of Government*, pp. 358–360 (Book II, Chapter 11, §§ 136–137).

[57] *Ibid.*

[58] *Ibid.*, p. 360 (Book II, Chapter 11, § 137).

to others' incalculable opinions – even when those others were thinking as hard and as rigorously as they could about natural law. The problem was that the Law of Nature was "unwritten, and so no where to be found but in the minds of Men,"[59] and in the mind of each person it depended on the particular path of reasoning that that person took. Locke was an opponent of innate ideas;[60] people had to figure this stuff out for themselves in real time; and if they figured it out for themselves what you would have in the first instance was a plethora of different results of that figuring. Your figuring might be different from my figuring, and, since this was not just a philosophical exercise, but one which was supposed to determine our individual rights, it might turn out that your view of the relation between your property and my property and your property and my interests, might be quite different from my view of the matter and quite different from the view of the next person I came across.[61]

The whole point of moving to a situation of positive law was to introduce some predictability into this natural law picture. But then that is why we want standing laws, publicly promulgated, that can attract the attention of us all – rather than rulers who just try to figure out for themselves case by case what the natural law requires. Unless we have an acknowledged body of positive laws known in advance to everyone – "stated

---

[59] *Ibid.*, pp. 350–351 (Book II, Chapter 9, § 124).

[60] John Locke, *An Essay Concerning Human Understanding* ed. P. H. Nidditch (Oxford: Oxford University Press, 1971), pp. 65 ff. (Book I, Chapter 3).

[61] See also the discussion in Jeremy Waldron, *The Dignity of Legislation* (Cambridge: Cambridge University Press, 1999), pp. 68 ff.

Rules of Right and Property to secure their Peace and Quiet …
[so] that … the People may know their Duty, and be safe and
secure within the limits of the Law"[62] – unless we have all that,
we are no better off than we would be in the state of nature,
where there was no telling whose natural law reasoning we
would suddenly find ourselves at the mercy of.

So far, so good: this is a powerful and compelling case
for the rule of positive law. But, having set out this constraint
on governance, which we recognize instantly as a Rule-of-Law
constraint, Locke immediately goes on to complicate matters –
in fact, I think he screws things up – by adding to it a substantive principle of respect for private property. He postulates as
one of his constraints on legislators that "[t]he Supream Power
cannot take from any Man any part of his Property without
his own consent."[63] And this, it seems, is supposed to be a substantive limit on what legislators may enact even when they
are complying with the formal constraints of clarity, stability,
and promulgation. They must rule by settled standing laws,
that is, by legislation known and publicized in advance, but
they may not rule by legislation that takes away the property
of the people.[64]

Now Locke acknowledges, as any sensible person
must, that government has to have the power of "the regulat-
ing of Property between the Subjects one amongst another"
and also that, since government is costly, "every one who
enjoys his share of the Protection, should pay out of his Estate

---

[62] Locke, *Two Treatises of Government*, pp. 359–360 (Book II, Chapter 11,
§ 137).

[63] *Ibid.*, p. 360 (Book II, Chapter 11, § 138).

[64] *Ibid.*, p. 412 (Book II, Chapter 19, § 222).

his proportion for the maintenance of it."[65] Those matters, as we know, are likely to be controversial – particularly as to the line between regulation and takings – and so they too need to be determined by settled standing laws, not by anyone's "unrestrain'd, and till that moment unknown Wills."

But then there is a more fundamental difficulty. The picture we are being sold has property rights being determined pre-politically; these are the ones that are to be respected by the legislature under this substantive constraint. But, though Locke gives us his own interesting theory of the pre-political generation of property rights – the so-called "Labour Theory," developed in Chapter 5 of the *Second Treatise*[66] – it is itself far from an uncontroversial theory. People in our day, as in his day, disagree about the rival claims of labor and occupancy, they disagree about the background of common ownership, they disagree about the provisos, about the introduction of money and the possibility of exchange, they disagree about how much anyone may appropriate by labor and how sensitive his appropriation must be to the impact on others. Above all, they disagree about the claims of welfare, need, and charity, on goods that others claim to have appropriated. We disagree about all that – in ways that were made evident, for example, in the debates about Nozick's book in the 1970s and in the subsequent literature on property.[67] And Locke and his contemporaries disagreed about all of this, and

[65] *Ibid.*, pp. 361–362 (Book ii, Chapter 11, § 139).
[66] *Ibid.*, pp. 286–291 (Book ii, Chapter 5, §§ 26–34).
[67] See e.g. Virginia Held, "Property Rights and Interests," *Social Research* 46 (1979), 577; and Thomas Scanlon, "Nozick on Rights, Liberty, and Property," *Philosophy and Public Affairs* 6 (1976), 3.

carried on disagreeing, even after Locke produced a remarkably interesting account.[68] And Locke knew, and signaled in a number of places that he knew, just how controversial this stuff was.[69]

By insisting therefore that positive law is subject to this substantive constraint rooted in the moral reality of pre-political property rights, Locke is subjecting the legislature to a discipline of uncertainty. The natural right of property is controversial; and so the administration of any substantive constraint of the Rule of Law along these lines is going to be controversial. This is particularly problematic inasmuch as Locke associates the substantive property constraint with the classic natural law position which holds that enactments violating the laws of nature have no validity.[70] The effect of this is that some people – let's say people who disagree with Locke about the claims of labor over occupancy – will disagree with him about which positive rules of property are valid and which are not. And similarly for those who disagree with him about the provisos, or about charity, or about money. In the state of nature, there is no telling whose reasoning on these matters

[68] James Tully, *A Discourse on Property: John Locke and his Adversaries* (Cambridge: Cambridge University Press, 1980), pp. 64 ff.
[69] See Waldron, *The Dignity of Legislation*, pp. 74–75.
[70] Locke, *Two Treatises of Government*, pp. 357–358 (Book II, Chapter 11, § 135): "Thus the law of nature stands as an eternal rule to all men, legislators as well as others. The rules that they make for other men's actions, must, as well as their own and other men's actions, be conformable to the law of nature, i.e. to the will of God, of which that is a declaration, and the fundamental law of nature being the preservation of mankind, no human sanction can be good, or valid against it."

one will be at the mercy of: one may be at the mercy of a John Locke or one may be at the mercy of a Samuel Pufendorf with a quite different theory.[71] And the move to civil society offers no help in this regard, since settled standing laws are now unsettled by a substantive constraint imposed upon positive law-making that ties them into these controversies.

In Chapter 2, I will be asking whether we can justify moving from a purely formal/procedural approach to the Rule of Law to *add in* a substantive conception. Can that addition be justified? But the upshot of this present discussion seems to be that, whatever the justification for the additional substantive constraint, what it does is *destabilize* the other elements of the Rule of Law. So we may find ourselves having to choose a stable conception of the Rule of Law which is mainly formal and procedural in character and an unstable one, with an element of substantive controversy added in.

There is a way out of this, but it won't be attractive to most latter-day Lockeans. James Tully, in a book published in 1980,[72] argued that Locke's substantive Rule-of-Law principle protected private property only in the sense of positive law rights of property already established by legislation. It was not supposed to protect natural law rights which, as Tully and I agree, were inherently controversial (even on Locke's own account). It was supposed to protect property inasmuch as property was already established by positive law.

---

[71] See e.g. Samuel Pufendorf, *On the Duty of Man and Citizen According to Natural Law*, ed. James Tully (Cambridge: Cambridge University Press), p. 85.

[72] Tully, *A Discourse on Property*, pp. 98 and 164–165.

When I was younger I wrote my doctoral dissertation on Locke and published several articles attacking Tully's interpretation.[73] I still think it is wrong, but I won't go into that now. The point is that Tully's maneuver saves the coherence of the position, but only by abandoning the claim that, for legal purposes, property is determined bottom-up on a private law basis in a way that is independent of legislation. On Tully's account, the property rights that are protected are themselves artifacts of public law. As such, they are clear, well known, and stable; and they are no longer at the mercy of natural law controversies. But the price of that deliverance is that the property rights in question, being the offspring of legislation, can have very little power and status to set up against legislation (of the environmental kind). Property is no longer privileged as a special or primeval form of law. It is just one set of laws among others. And we judge it, in its relation to public policy, and in its relation to other laws, without assuming its untouchability.

And that, it seems to me is the counsel of wisdom. It is better in the end to evaluate laws on their own merits – and to make whatever case can be made about the exigencies of market economy untrammeled by too much regulation – better to make that case directly, rather than muddy the waters by pretending that some laws have transcendent status under the auspices of the Rule of Law and that other laws – like environmental regulations – barely qualify for legal respect at all.

[73] See Waldron, "Locke, Tully and the Regulation of Property"; and also Jeremy Waldron, *The Right to Private Property* (Oxford: Clarendon Press, 1990), pp. 232–241.

2

A substantive Rule of Law?

Some people think that the Rule of Law is a purely formal/procedural ideal, neutral as between different kinds of law, provided that the law to whatever ends it is directed satisfies formal constraints of generality, prospectivity, clarity, etc., and is applied in a procedurally fair and respectable manner.

Others, however, believe in a substantive dimension for the Rule of Law and, of these, there are some who believe that there is a special affinity between the Rule of Law and the vindication and support of private property rights. Those who take this view believe that the Rule of Law looks with a jaundiced eye, rather than a neutral eye, on legislation of the kind we are considering – the conservation statute, for example, that was at stake in *Lucas* v. *South Carolina Coastal Council* in 1992. It is part of the mission of the Rule of Law, on this account, to support private property; so, to that extent, the Rule of Law provides a basis for criticizing legislative intervention. In Chapter 1, I associated something approaching this position with theorists like Richard Epstein, F. A. Hayek, and John Locke.

The Lockean view was of particular interest to us in Chapter 1, because it continues to influence the thought of modern jurists like Richard Epstein. Epstein has identified an important contrast in the ways that people think about the relation between law and property. Some see property as the child of law, the artifact of positive law-making. On this view, "property rights are arbitrary assemblages of rights that the state creates for its own instrumental purposes, and which it can undo almost at will for the same instrumental ends."[1] But that is not the view that Epstein favors. He says that no sensible view of ownership, "[n]o system of property rights rests on the premise that the state may bestow or deny rights in things to private persons on whatever terms it sees fit. Rather, the correct starting point is the Lockean position that property rights come from the bottom up."[2]

At the very least, Epstein says, we should associate the Rule of Law with private law values, organizing our understanding of the Rule of Law so that it looks much more askance at the operation of public law. I don't think anyone has ever thought (and I don't think Epstein thought) that it is plausible to associate the Rule of Law *exclusively* with the vindication of private law rights. An awful lot of the work that the Rule of Law does, it does with special emphasis on criminal law, in the principle of legality for example, or in the special emphasis on prospectivity in criminal law. (In the United States, the constitutional prohibition on *ex post facto* law-making has no operation at all outside the area of criminal law.)[3] But much of that work is negative, trying to rein in public law or blunt the force of its impact upon us, and it might be thought, by those in the Lockean tradition, that this is consistent with a special connection between the Rule of Law and the *affirmative* support and vindication of private law rights of property.

---

[1] R.A. Epstein, *Design for Liberty: Private Property, Public Administration and the Rule of Law* (Cambridge, MA: Harvard University Press, 2011), p. 63.

[2] *Ibid.*, p. 99.

[3] See *Calder* v. *Bull*, 3 US 386 (1798). See also the discussion in L.F. Fuller, *The Morality of Law*, pp. 57–59.

But, in the end, I don't think this is going to work. It is partly because I share Hans Kelsen's skepticism about the very basis of the distinction between private law and public law.[4] All law involves something like state agency, if only because in the end it is the state that is called upon to come to the aid of private litigants in upholding their private law rights. Moreover, I don't think that devotion to the Rule-of-Law ideal should lead us to neglect or denigrate the role of human agency involved in both law-making and law-enforcement. I will talk more about this in Chapter 3. Law works more than ever these days as an integrated whole, so that we think of private law as serving public as well as private purposes and as being on that account naturally susceptible to public law emendation, and the rights it comprises being subject to both extension and restriction for public purposes. This is true in tort law, it is true in contracts, and there is no reason to insist that it cannot be true in property law. There is no turning back to an era where the private law relations could be conceived in a purely formalist way and understood in a way that was purged of any possible public policy understanding.

***

The failure of the Lockean maneuver and the public law/private law maneuver does not mean that we have refuted the claim that private property commands a special place in the ideal of the Rule of Law. There may be other ways of vindicating the sort of connection that Epstein, Hayek, and others are interested in.

---

[4] See Hans Kelsen, *The Pure Theory of Law* (Gloucester, MA: Peter Smith, 1989), pp. 281–284.

Academics who work in the shadow of Albert Venn Dicey, Lon Fuller, and Joseph Raz, tend to think of the Rule of Law in formal and procedural terms. Laws should be clear, public, and prospective, they should take the form of stable and learnable rules, they should be administered fairly and impartially, they should operate as limits on state action, and they should apply equally to each and every person, no matter how rich and powerful they are. That's the formal/procedural conception. But there has long been a debate about whether the Rule of Law also has, or requires, a substantive dimension.

Many good-hearted people believe that it should. For example, it is widely believed that "a system of positive law that fails to respect core human rights ... does not deserve to be called a rule of law system."[5] The World Justice Council quotes Arthur Chaskalson, former Chief Justice of South Africa, to this effect:

> [T]he apartheid government, its officers and agents were accountable in accordance with the laws; the laws were clear; publicized, and stable, and were upheld by law enforcement officials and judges. What was missing was the substantive component of the rule of law. The process by which the laws were made was not fair (only whites, a minority of the population, had the vote). And the laws themselves were not fair. They institutionalized discrimination, vested broad discretionary powers in the executive, and failed to protect fundamental rights.

[5] Mark David Agrast, Juan Carlos Botero, and Alejandro Ponce, *Rule of Law Index 2011* (Washington, DC: World Justice Project, 2011), p. 12, available at http://worldjusticeproject.org/rule-of-law-index/index-2011.

THE RULE OF LAW

Without a substantive content there would be no answer
to the criticism, sometimes voiced, that the rule of law is
"an empty vessel into which any law could be poured."[6]

I said in Chapter 1 that Joseph Raz is famous for insisting that
"the rule of law is just one of the virtues which a legal system may possess and by which it is to be judged," and that
we should not try to read into it other considerations about
democracy, human rights, and social justice.[7] Those considerations, he said, are better understood as independent dimensions of assessment. Tom Bingham, however, in his book on
The Rule of Law, said this in response to Raz:

> While ... one can recognize the logical force of
> Professor Raz's contention, I would roundly reject it in
> favor of a "thick" definition, embracing the protection of
> human rights within its scope. A state which
> savagely represses or persecutes sections of its people
> cannot in my view be regarded as observing the rule of
> law, even if the transport of the persecuted minority to
> the concentration camp or the compulsory exposure of
> female children on the mountainside is the subject of
> detailed laws duly enacted and scrupulously
> observed.[8]

Lord Bingham's position has an intuitive appeal, even if it irri-
tates in its casual rejection of a point whose logic it claims to
recognize.

---

[6] Remarks at the World Justice Forum 1, held in Vienna, Austria, in July
2008, quoted *ibid.*, p. 9.

[7] Raz, "The Rule of Law and Its Virtue," p. 211.

[8] Bingham, *The Rule of Law*, p. 67.

Both Chaskalson and Bingham seem to want to fill out the formal/procedural conception of the Rule of Law with some human rights component. And many liberals are inclined to follow them in that. But this is not the only possibility. I have argued elsewhere for an association of the Rule of Law with prohibitions on torture, brutality, and degradation – a specific subset of human rights.[9] Many associate it with a presumption of liberty or a presumption in favor of human dignity. (I have argued this also.)[10] Others – and Arthur Chaskalson hinted at this – associate the Rule of Law with a substantive dimension of democracy. And, of course, there is the possibility that we are investigating – that the substantive dimension of the Rule of Law is some role in the special protection of private property.

All this sounds an interesting danger signal. Once we open up the possibility of the Rule of Law having a substantive dimension and not just being a collection of formal and procedural principles, we inaugurate a sort of competition whereby everyone clamors to have their favorite value, their favorite political ideal, incorporated as a substantive dimension of the Rule of Law. Those who favor property rights and market economy will no doubt scramble to privilege their favorite values in this regard. But so will those who favor

[9] Jeremy Waldron, "Torture and Positive Law: Jurisprudence for the White House," *Columbia Law Review* 105 (2005), 1681, pp. 1726–1728, reprinted in Jeremy Waldron, *Torture, Terror, and Trade-offs: Philosophy for the White House* (Oxford: Oxford University Press, 2010), pp. 232–234.

[10] See Jeremy Waldron, "How Law Protects Dignity," *Cambridge Law Review* (2012), forthcoming, available at http://ssrn.com/abstract=1973341.

human rights, or those who favor democratic participation, or those who favor civil liberties or social justice. The result in my view is likely to be a general decline in political articulacy, as people struggle to use the same term to express disparate ideals.

It is not quite a zero-sum game. Bingham in his discussion thinks that if property comes in at all it comes in under the auspices of human rights, because it is mentioned in Article 1 of the First Protocol to the European Convention on Human Rights. And there is, I guess, no reason why the Rule of Law shouldn't have several substantive dimensions. In fact, once one abandons any Razian inhibition, maybe we should just say: "Bring 'em on! The more the merrier."

But it really isn't clear how one goes about arguing for the recognition of a substantive dimension. How can one show that private property has (or doesn't have) a special importance in this regard? We are after all talking about the shape of our political ideas, and, since these are not ordained canonically for us, it may be thought that we can divide them up any way we like and that there is no correct or incorrect way of limiting or extending the application of an ideal such as the Rule of Law. There are only pragmatic and utilitarian arguments about the economy of theorizing; and those are likely to be pretty thin.[11] I know comparable questions arise about our definition of "democracy" – how much human rights baggage does that term convey? They arise too in our discussion of "liberty" – how far does that ideal, particularly

---

[11] But see the appeal to exactly these values, in defending a broad definition of "law" in Hart, *The Concept of Law*, pp. 209–210.

in its positive form, commit us to a whole vision of social order? And in our discussion of "justice": was Rawls right to encompass within the concept of justice a whole vision of a well-ordered society, or should justice have been conceived more narrowly than that? "Liberty," justice, "democracy," and "the Rule of Law" – these are just words for various segments of our political morality and presumably we can organize the categories any way we like. Perhaps there is little point in insisting on any particular segmentation. Unless we are committed to a strong Platonic sense of what each one entails, the reasons we are going to have to appeal are reasons having to do with the pragmatics of argumentation – that dividing the concepts up in such and such a way makes us more articulate, makes it easier for us to separate distinct lines of argument, or makes it easier to spot equivocations and to grasp and face up to the need for trade-offs.

Sometimes the case that is made is quite cynical, involving what the emotivist philosopher, Charles Stevenson, would have recognized as a "persuasive definition."[12] Certain hard-nosed World Bank types say, in effect, that our real interest is in getting governments to respect property rights, investor concerns, and the principle of free markets, and we should use whatever means come to hand to promote these ideals. "Because the phrase 'rule of law' has acquired such a strong positive connotation," it may be useful in this regard. Since everyone happens to be in favor of the Rule of Law at the moment, we can use the good vibrations associated with the phrase to bolster the case that is made for the Washington

[12]   C. L. Stevenson, "Persuasive Definitions," *Mind* 47 (1938), 331.

consensus and drive home its points about markets and property.[13] This is calculated – indeed manipulated – as a purely instrumental case for using the phrase in a certain way.[14] It is said that "[w]hat we really should be interested in – that is, the essence of the rule of law – is the substantive or functional outcome. Whether or not the formal characteristics contribute to that outcome ought to be a matter for research, not presumption."[15]

Are there more respectable ways of proceeding? I can think of several. One is to bring to the surface the values that motivate the traditional formal/procedural aspects of the Rule of Law. After all, we don't insist on clarity, generality, publicity, prospectivity, and due process for their own sake; we do so because of the way they serve liberty or (in Fuller's account and in Raz's account) because of the way they enable law to respect human dignity.[16] But I am not sure that this is going

---

[13] See e.g. Matthew Stephenson, "Rule of Law as a Goal of Development Policy" (Washington, DC: World Bank Research, n.d.) available at http://go.worldbank.org/DZETJ85MD0 (last visited December 27, 2011): "The main advantage of the substantive version of the rule of law is the explicit equation of the rule of law with something normatively good and desirable. The rule of law is good in this case because it is defined as such. This is appealing, first because the subjective judgment is made explicit rather than hidden in formal criteria, and, second, because the phrase 'rule of law' has acquired such a strong positive connotation." I have discussed this further in Jeremy Waldron, "Legislation and the Rule of Law," *Legisprudence* 1 (2007), 91, p. 118.

[14] Stephenson, "Rule of Law as a Goal of Development Policy."

[15] *Ibid.*

[16] Raz, "The Rule of Law and Its Virtue," p. 221: "[O]bservance of the rule of law is necessary if the law is to respect human dignity. Respecting human dignity entails treating humans as persons capable of planning

to get us to anything like private property as a substantive dimension of the Rule of Law. The substantive values yielded by this approach are likely to be quite abstract: liberty, equality, and dignity, rather than particular values like the principle of private property.

***

The other possibility is to see if we can discern a substantive dimension for the Rule of Law by considering the substantive tendency of some of the acknowledged formal and procedural elements. What I mean is that certain features of the formal/ procedural account may point us in the direction of certain substantive values, imparting a certain momentum which may carry us in a particular substantive direction. For example, the Rule-of-Law requirement of generality may point us in the direction of justice: by insisting that like cases be treated alike, it sets us off down the road of considering substantively which cases ought to be considered (and treated) alike.[17] Or the Rule-of-Law requirement of prospectivity may set us off in the direction of privileging human agency and planning; it may, to that extent, put us on the road to a substantive link between the Rule of Law and individual autonomy. I am not saying that, in these cases, the momentum is irresistible, only that it is there and it seems to furnish an obvious basis for arguing in favor of a substantive dimension. I think this is quite promising as a strategy. Let me talk for a few pages about a particularly powerful version of it.

and plotting their future. Thus, respecting people's dignity includes respecting their autonomy, their right to control their future."

[17] See also the remarks on generality in Hart, *The Concept of Law*, pp. 157–167.

One important aspect of the Rule of Law as it is traditionally conceived is the requirement that the laws be reasonably stable. This is a hardy perennial. Aristotle emphasized it in Book ii of the *Politics*, when he suggested that, by and large, change in the laws was a bad thing, since it undermines their role in the inculcation of virtue.[18] That is hardly our concern today. Today, the explanation for the importance of legal stability is probably the one stated by Joseph Raz:

> If [the laws] are frequently changed people will find it difficult to find out what the law is at any given moment and will be constantly in fear that the law has been changed since they last learnt what it was.[19]

Not only that, but it is also important to extend the horizon of action:

> [P]eople need to know the law not only for short-term decisions … but also for long-term planning. Knowledge of at least the general outlines and sometimes even of details of tax law and company law are often important for business plans which will bear fruit only years later. Stability is essential if people are to be guided by law in their long-term decisions.[20]

It is, said Raz in 1977, a matter of dignity: "Respecting human dignity entails treating humans as persons capable of planning and plotting their future."[21]

---

[18] Aristotle, *Politics*, pp. 81–83 (Book ii, Chapter 8).
[19] Raz, "The Rule of Law and Its Virtue," p. 214.
[20] *Ibid.*, pp. 214–215.   [21] *Ibid.*, p. 221.

These are general reasons for stability, arising out of the need for individuals to be able to guide their actions, short- medium- and long-term actions, on the basis of a secure knowledge of the law.[22] Now, on the face of it, these reasons apply to laws of every kind, whether criminal law, commercial law, public regulation, tax law, or aspects of private law, such as tort or contract. People need to know where they stand; they need to be able to plan around the law's demands in the autonomous organization of their lives. Since law's presence in people's lives tends to be intrusive if not coercive, it is important that its presence be made calculable, so that it can enter into their planning. And, since other people's actions may also impact intrusively upon us, we need to know in advance how, and to what extent, these too will be controlled by law.

We need, in short, a basis for expectation. Now in jurisprudence, the best account that was ever given of the importance of legal expectations was given more than 150 years ago by the utilitarian philosopher, Jeremy Bentham, in a work entitled *Principles of the Civil Code*.[23] Expectation, said Bentham, is

---

[22] In Chapter 3, I shall have something to say about the limits of this principle given some of the features that modern legal systems possess. See also Jeremy Waldron, "Thoughtfulness and the Rule of Law," *British Academy Review* 18 (2011), 1; this is also available at http://ssrn.com/abstract=1759550.

[23] Jeremy Bentham, "Principles of the Civil Code," in Jeremy Bentham, *The Theory of Legislation*, ed. C. K. Ogden (London: Kegan Paul, Trench, Trubner & Co., 1931), p. 88. There is a useful and accessible excerpt from this in C. B. Macpherson (ed.), *Property: Mainstream and Critical Positions* (Oxford: Basil Blackwell, 1978), p. 41. But I shall cite the 1931 Ogden edition.

immeasurably important in human affairs. It "is a chain which unites our present existence to our future existence."

> It is hence that we have the power of forming a general plan
> of conduct; it is hence that the successive instants which
> compose the duration of life are not isolated and independent
> points, but become continuous parts of a whole.[24]

The establishment of expectations, said Bentham, is largely the work of law, and the principle of secure expectations, what he called the principle of security, is a vital constraint on the action of law: "The principle of security ... requires that events, so far as they depend upon laws, should conform to the expectations which law itself has created."[25]

So far, this is just about legal stability in general. But it is not hard to see how someone might think this interest in security, secure expectations, has a special relation to property. And that was exactly Jeremy Bentham's position in the *Principles of the Civil Code*. I am going to quote quite extensively:

> The idea of property consists in an established expectation;
> in the persuasion of being able to draw such or such an
> advantage from the thing possessed ... [T]his expectation,
> this persuasion, can only be the work of law. I cannot
> count upon the enjoyment of that which I regard as mine,
> except through the promise of the law which guarantees
> it to me. It is law alone which permits me to forget my
> natural weakness. It is only through the protection of law
> that I am able to inclose a field, and to give myself up to its
> cultivation with the sure though distant hope of harvest.[26]

[24] Bentham, "Principles of the Civil Code," p. 111.
[25] *Ibid.*   [26] *Ibid.*, p. 112.

Now it is important to understand that Bentham had no patience at all with Locke's theory of natural property rights. I might appropriate something, he said, and hope to hang on to it outside the auspices of positive law, but "[h]ow miserable and precarious is such a possession!"

> A feeble and momentary expectation may result from time to time from circumstances purely physical; but a strong and permanent expectation can result only from law … Property and law are born together, and die together. Before laws were made there was no property; take away laws, and property ceases.[27]

When we made this point against Locke, the inference was that property can be manipulated by law, can be modified, and must be responsive to law's ever-changing constitutive and regulatory demands. But Bentham drives the point in the opposite direction. Precisely because property is the product of law, we need a special jurisprudential doctrine to stabilize it. Otherwise, it will become law's plaything. And the doctrine that Bentham favors is utterly conservative:

> As regards property, security consists in receiving no check, no shock, no derangement to the expectation founded on the laws, of enjoying such and such a portion of good. The legislator owes the greatest respect to this expectation which he has himself produced.[28]

In this way, the protection of property rights emerges as a substantive theme in a process that began from simply noting the human interest in the stability of the laws that is protected by

27 *Ibid.*, p. 113.   28 *Ibid.*

traditional formal and procedural principles of the Rule of Law. That, it seems to me, as far as it goes, is a good and respectable way to argue for a substantive version of the Rule of Law.

Similar variations on the human need for legal stability may also be in play here. In the tradition of David Hume, people might point to special considerations about the personal and psychological investment that an individual has in the objects connected to him. "What has long lain under our eye," said Hume in Book III of the *Treatise*, "and has often been employ'd to our advantage, that we are always the most unwilling to part with; but can easily live without possessions, which we never have enjoy'd, and are not accustom'd to."[29]

> Such is the effect of custom, that it not only reconciles us to anything we have long enjoy'd, but even gives us an affection for it, and makes us prefer it to other objects, which may be more valuable, but are less known to us.[30]

Bentham thought along the same lines:

> Everything which I possess, or to which I have a title, I consider in my own mind as destined always to belong to me. I make it the basis of my expectations, and of the hopes of those dependent upon me; and I form my plan of life accordingly ... [O]ur property becomes a part of our being, and cannot be torn from us without rending us to the quick.[31]

---

[29] David Hume, *A Treatise of Human Nature*, ed. L. A. Selby-Bigge and P. H. Nidditch (Oxford: Clarendon Press, 1978), p. 503 (Book III, Part ii, section 3).

[30] *Ibid.*

[31] Bentham, "Principles of the Civil Code," p. 115.

Someone who has been designated officially as the owner of a given piece of land has actual control of it as often as not. He will know it intimately, he may inhabit it with his family, cultivate it, earn his living from it, care about it, and regard it as part of the wealth that he relies on for his own security and that of his descendants. He will be able to point to features of the land where his work and his initiative have made a difference, so that the land will not only seem like his, but actually seem to be part of himself. These effects are likely to accrue to him by virtue of the operation of the system of property as positive law quite independently of whether it is just or unjust, or whether he or anyone else regards it as just or unjust.[32]

And the thought is echoed by a modern jurist, Margaret Radin, who has argued, in a number of influential articles, that respect for existing property rights is bound up with respect for persons:

> Most people possess certain objects they feel are almost part of themselves. These objects are closely bound up with personhood because they are part of the way we constitute ourselves as continuing personal entities in the world.[33]

There is, as I said, a sort of natural continuity between these accounts of property and the Razian explanation of the

---

[32] See also the discussion in Jeremy Waldron, "Property, Honesty, and Normative Resilience," in Stephen Munzer (ed.), *New Essays in the Legal and Political Theory of Property* (Cambridge: Cambridge University Press, 2001), p. 10.

[33] Margaret Jane Radin, "Property and Personhood," reprinted in her collection, *Reinterpreting Property* (Chicago: University of Chicago Press, 1993), p. 36.

importance of relative stability in terms of the dignity of man as a being who lives, acts, and plans in the world over long periods of time – a natural momentum that seems to set us off down this substantive road.

**

However, there is a catch. It is not at all clear that an argument of this kind privileges *private* property – specifically rights of ownership – in the sense that (say) Richard Epstein has in mind. After all, property rights come in all shapes and sizes – the rights of full ownership, the respective rights of landlords and tenants, and long-term leasehold rights, not to mention the rights of the members of a property-owning collective, the rights of owners-in-common, and so on. I mentioned Margaret Radin's position. Radin uses the idea of respect for established expectations to distinguish between the claims of landlords and the claims of tenants in disputes about residential rent control.[34] On the powerful account she provides, it is the tenant, not the owner, who is invested psychologically in the stability of the property relation. Someone like Epstein might expect an argument connecting the Rule of Law with property to privilege the property rights of the landlord. But he might be disappointed.

Property is not the same as private ownership, and an account that privileges property under the auspices of the Rule of Law may be hospitable to other types of property relation as well. In a famous coda on the Rule of Law at the end of his book, *Whigs and Hunters*, the late E. P. Thompson reminded us that, in battles between eighteenth-century agribusiness

---

[34] Margaret Jane Radin, "Residential Rent Control," in Radin, *Reinterpreting Property*, p. 72.

and eighteenth-century eco-terrorists, the conflict was not just property against humanity: "[I]t was alternative definitions of property-rights: for the landowner, enclosure–for the cottager, common rights; for the forest officialdom, 'preserved grounds' for the deer; for the foresters, the right to take turfs."[35] People invest themselves in property rights of all kinds and it is by no means clear that, in confrontations between owners and those who stand up for various kinds of public right, the Rule of Law, on the conception we are considering, will always side with the owner. A public footpath may have been defined for centuries across a patch of what is otherwise a privately owned field. People in the neighborhood might have just as much investment in the security of their footpath – in the expectation they have of being able to use it when they want – and the plans that they build around this expectation as the farmer does in his ownership of the field and in his view that he ought to be able to plough and cultivate it in a regular pattern unconstrained by the public right of way.

The point is acknowledged most clearly by Bentham. As his discussion of security and property draws to a close, Bentham begins his conclusion with what sounds like a traditional privileging of unequal property:

> In consulting the grand principle of security, what ought the legislator to decree respecting the mass of property already existing? He ought to maintain the distribution as it is actually established.[36]

[35] E. P. Thompson, *Whigs and Hunters: The Origin of the Black Act* (Harmondsworth: Penguin Books, 1975), p. 261.
[36] Bentham, "Principles of the Civil Code," p. 119.

But then, for the purposes of those who want to privilege private property, Bentham takes a radically wrong step. He says that the principle of respecting the existing distribution is "a general and simple rule which applies itself to all states; and which adapts itself to all places, even those of the most opposite character."

> There is nothing more different than the state of property in America, in England, in Hungary, and in Russia. Generally, in the first of these countries, the cultivator is a proprietor; in the second, a tenant; in the third, attached to the glebe; in the fourth, a slave. However, the supreme principle of security commands the preservation of all these distributions, though their nature is so different, and though they do not produce the same sum of happiness.[37]

It seems like a wrong step, but in fact it is Bentham following the logic of his own position. Maybe there are certain property systems that find it harder than others to get a foothold in human expectation. There are certain laws, he says, which "lie under a sort of natural incapacity of being made known to the people; they refuse to take hold of the memory."[38] And there is no doubt that in some of his exposition his account of security is biased towards the good husbandry of a private proprietor. But Bentham is honest enough to see that his account can be generalized in all sorts of directions. Maybe the law that secures the beaches and the coastline

---

[37] *Ibid.*

[38] Jeremy Bentham, "Supply without Burthen or Escheat *vice* Taxation," in *Jeremy Bentham's Economic Writings*, ed. W. Stark (London: George, Allen and Unwin, 1952), vol. I, p. 321.

in *Lucas* v. *South Carolina Coastal Council* is as invested in protecting the expectations of holidaymakers on the Isle of Palms, for example, as in protecting the expectations associated with Mr. Lucas's real estate investments. At best, we circle back to the general argument for legal stability, not for an argument that privileges the stability of private property as opposed to stability in other areas of law.

***

The word "property" was only beginning to emerge in its modern meaning in the seventeenth century, when John Locke wrote about the topic.[39] And we know that he often signaled his desire to use the term in a broad sense, encompassing life and liberty as well as specific interest in (say) real estate.[40] This is partly a matter of semantics, of how the meaning of the word "property" evolved, from a broader to a narrower sense. But it also reminds us of an important substantive point about property, that the functions it performs – providing individuals with security and a stable horizon for their expectations – can be performed by other aspects of law as well.

One of the theorists most associated in the public mind (to the extent that the public thinks about these things at all) with a property-oriented account of the Rule of Law is Friedrich Hayek. But even Hayek acknowledges that the security and independence that historically has been associated with property is in the modern world associated with much more diverse and complex legal structures and

---

[39] See Peter Laslett, "Introduction" to Locke, *Two Treatises of Government*, p. 101.
[40] Locke, *Two Treatises of Government*, p. 341 (Book II, Chapter VII, § 87).

THE RULE OF LAW

arrangements – many of them contractual in character. In *The Constitution of Liberty*, Hayek spoke of the need to guarantee for each individual a sphere of freedom where he could pursue his own interest without coercive interference.[41] Traditionally, this might be understood in terms of property – something like "an Englishman's home is his castle," and he can organize things within his castle as he pleases. We have all sorts of public law problems with this, once we begin to understand the violent and oppressive things that sometimes go on inside the gates of people's castles. But, even leaving that important point aside, Hayek is not prepared to accept that private property on the castle analogy is the only way of securing individual freedom. "In modern society," he says, "the essential requisite for the protection of the individual against coercion is not that he possess property," but that he have multiple possibilities of access to "the material means which enable him to pursue a plan of action."

> It is one of the accomplishments of modern society that freedom may be enjoyed by a person with practically no property of his own … That other people's property can be serviceable in the achievement of our aims is due mainly to the enforceability of contracts. The whole network of rights created by contracts is as important a part of our own protected sphere, [and] as much the basis of our plans, as any property of our own.[42]

Once again, it seems to follow that we should be sticking with the general Rule-of-Law commitment to stability such as it is,

[41] Hayek, *The Constitution of Liberty*, pp. 139–140.
[42] *Ibid.*, pp. 140–141.

rather than looking specifically to its association with one limited domain of law namely private property.

Hayek's case still leaves individual security in the
domain of private law. But the point can be extended in a
public law direction as well. In 1970, in the case of *Goldberg
v. Kelly*,[43] the Supreme Court of the United States held that an
entitlement to welfare support could not just be taken away
from a needy individual without explanation and without a
hearing affording him an opportunity to state his side of the
case. In the course of that decision, the Court said this:

> Much of the existing wealth in this country takes the form
> of rights that do not fall within traditional common-law
> concepts of property. It has been aptly noted that "[s]ociety
> today is built around entitlement. The automobile dealer
> has his franchise, the doctor and lawyer their professional
> licenses, the worker his union membership, contract,
> and pension rights, the executive his contract and stock
> options; all are devices to aid security and independence.
> Many of the most important of these entitlements now flow
> from government: subsidies to farmers and businessmen,
> routes for airlines and channels for television stations; long
> term contracts for defense, space, and education; social
> security pensions for individuals. Such sources of security,
> whether private or public, are no longer regarded as
> luxuries or gratuities; to the recipients they are essentials,
> fully deserved, and in no sense a form of charity. It is only
> the poor whose entitlements, although recognized by
> public policy, have not been effectively enforced."[44]

[43] *Goldberg* v. *Kelly*, 397 US 254 (1970).
[44] *Ibid.*, p. 263, n. 8 (Brennan J., for the Court).

The Court was quoting from an article published in 1964 by Charles Reich, a Yale law professor, entitled "The New Property." Reich had argued that:

> [o]ne of the most important developments in the United States has been the emergence of government as a major source of wealth. Government is a gigantic syphon. It draws in revenue and power, and pours forth wealth: money, benefits, services, contracts, franchises, and licenses. Government has always had this function. But while in early times it was minor, today's distribution of largess is on a vast, imperial scale. The valuables dispensed by government take many forms, but they all share one characteristic. They are steadily taking the place of traditional forms of wealth – forms which are held as private property. Social insurance substitutes for savings; a government contract replaces a businessman's customers and goodwill. The wealth of more and more Americans depends upon a relationship to government … As government largess has grown in importance, quite naturally there has been pressure for the protection of individual interests in it. The holder of a broadcast license or a motor carrier permit or a grazing permit for the public lands tends to consider this wealth his "own," and to seek legal protection against interference with his enjoyment.[45]

It is a powerful and important argument, and, again, there is no serious possibility of rolling this back. So, if we are really to pay attention to the security of expectation that individuals

[45] Charles Reich, "The New Property," *Yale Law Journal* 73 (1964), 733, pp. 739–740.

need in the autonomous conduct of their lives, if that is the substantive direction in which the formal requirements of the Rule of Law steer us, then we have to think also about the guarantees that are associated with these new forms of "property" too and that means guarantees in relation to public as well as private provision, or guarantees in relation to the stability of public licensing and regulation.

Now these are certainly worthy aims. But, as we saw in the case of Bentham, they mean that the ideal of security no longer takes us from the Rule of Law to *private* property; it takes us from the Rule of Law to law in all its varieties inasmuch as it impacts on the free conduct of our lives and to the provision of the space we need for autonomous engagement in economic activity. It takes us from the Rule of Law to property in a sense that cannot be confined to the private property interests that are the subject of our discussion.

***

Let us pause and take stock. We have been examining the possibility of establishing a special connection between the Rule of Law and private property *via* the stabilization and securing of expectation, which is an aim that seems to be common between the two. And our argument has been that such an argument seems to prove a lot more than the defenders of private property want, since it directs our attention to a myriad of areas in which this security is important, not all of which involve private ownership as it is ordinarily conceived. That said, the argument just made does not entirely discredit the link with private property. It still leaves Mr. Lucas with his beachfront lots on Beechwood East on the Isle of Palms saying: "Well, whatever the situation with Bentham's views on other forms of property, or Hayekian contracts or Reich's new property, I, at least, am relying on a traditional package of real estate so far as my expectations are concerned. Other kinds of rights may also be privileged. But that doesn't mean mine are not. So I at least ought to be sheltered by any generally available legal security from the sort of upset that was served on me by regulations made under the Beachfront Management Act." It seems reasonable for Mr. Lucas to say something like that.

I will talk a bit in general terms about the legal security Mr. Lucas craved in Chapter 3. But now, let me say something about a further difficulty that arises when we try to give this real-estate developer the benefit of a special Rule-of-Law doctrine so far as his traditional private property is concerned.

No one in the modern debate about property needs to be told that, from a legal point of view, ownership is not a single right but comprises a bundle of rights, of various Hohfeldian shapes and various sizes.[46] An owner of land characteristically has the privilege of using the land, the right that others not come on it or use it without his permission, the power to alienate it completely through gift or sale, or in part, or for a period by leasing it, the liability to have it seized by creditors in the event of unpaid debt or bankruptcy, and so on.[47]

Property may represent a unified idea, but when we are exploring its legal ramifications we have to pay attention to the detail. So, for example, in American takings law, there is often a

---

[46] See Wesley N. Hohfeld, *Fundamental Legal Conceptions* (New Haven, CT: Yale University Press, 1919).

[47] The best analysis is still A. M. Honoré, "Ownership," in A. G. Guest (ed.), *Oxford Essays in Jurisprudence* (Oxford: Oxford University Press, 1961), pp. 112–128.

question about which sticks in an owner's bundle of rights are impacted or broken by some offending statute or regulation. In *Lucas v. South Carolina Coastal Council*, the majority held that a restriction on use that drastically reduced the likely resale value that the owner was anticipating amounted more or less to a taking of the whole thing. They quoted Coke, who asked: "[F]or what is the land but the profit thereof?"[48] But other justices on the panel disagreed. Justice Blackmun insisted that the

> Petitioner still can enjoy other attributes of ownership, such as the right to exclude others, "one of the most essential sticks in the bundle of rights that are commonly characterized as property." Petitioner can picnic, swim, camp in a tent, or live on the property in a movable trailer … Petitioner also retains the right to alienate the land, which would have value for neighbors and for those prepared to enjoy proximity to the ocean without a house.[49]

[48] Edward Coke, *Institutes of the Laws of England*, in Steve Sheppard (ed.), *The Selected Writings of Sir Edward Coke*, vol. II, p. 609.

[49] *Lucas v. South Carolina Coastal Council*, 505 US 1003, pp. 1043–1044 (Blackmun J., dissenting). It appears that, during oral argument, the justices pursued this theme:

CHIEF JUSTICE REHNQUIST: Is it perfectly clear … that [the petitioner] … was denied all economically viable use of his land?
MR. LEWIS [counsel for Lucas]: Yes, sir.
JUSTICE WHITE: So you feel it was completely worthless.
MR. LEWIS: Yes, sir.
JUSTICE WHITE: Would you be willing to give it to me?
MR. LEWIS: I don't own it, but with the taxes that are owed on it I would be willing to give it to you, yes, sir. (Laughter.)

See the transcript available at www.oyez.org/cases/1990-1999/1991/1991_91_453.

The issue there is inescapable. The Constitution prohibits legislative takings, but, since regulative legislation tends to impact on some rights and not others, we have to ask in detail which impacts amount in effect to a taking of the whole thing and which do not.

Is the same true when we are exploring the relation between private property and a political ideal? Can we say, as political philosophers, that the Rule of Law just protects private property without saying what *aspects* of private property it protects? I am not sure. The idea of the Rule of Law's having a special role to play in the protection of private property is perhaps not beset in the same way with doctrinal rigidities or with the conundrums that constitutional law throws up. No particular official consequence follows from anyone's determination that the Rule of Law does or does not protect a given incident of property. Yet, if our political morality is not to fall into incoherence, there must be something to be said on this issue – that is, if we want to maintain a belief that the Rule of Law privileges and protects property rights.

In my book, *The Right to Private Property*, published a long time ago, I said that we should not let the intricacies of the bundle theory blind us to the importance of private property as a general, intuitive idea, and that we should distinguish between the concept of private property and various conceptions of private property, with the conceptions being spelled out in terms of various configurations of the bundle.[50] So

[50] Waldron, *The Right to Private Property*, pp. 47–53, drawing on Bruce Ackerman, *Private Property and the Constitution* (New Haven, CT: Yale University Press, 1977), pp. 97–98.

maybe the alleged connection that we are in pursuit of is just a connection between the Rule of Law and the *concept* of private property rather than between the Rule of Law and the bundle of rights specified in any particular conception of ownership.

That's possible, but then it leaves the owner of those beachfront lots on the Isle of Palms in a rather invidious position, because, as the dissenters said in *Lucas*, he is still the owner of those lots. The ownership has not been taken away from him, or, if it has, it is so only on the basis of a particular controversial conception of ownership. Someone might argue that in the intuitive sense it is still his property.

I don't mean that as a sneaky academic maneuver. The fact is that in the modern world even our intuitive sense of what it is to be the owner of something has to be an adaptable one. In rather the same way in which we come to identify our personal income in terms of post-deduction payment, net of income tax – this is argued in a book by Liam Murphy and Thomas Nagel, called *The Myth of Ownership: Taxes and Justice*[51] – so also it is arguable that people nowadays identify their property in a way that takes net account of actual and sometimes likely restrictions on use and development. Every owner of property in a historic town center is familiar with this, and it is not at all clear why we should have to work with an intuitive notion of property that stands aloof from this awareness. These days, any farmer or any real-estate developer understands this. They may wish that things were different, but that is a political aim, not necessarily bound up with the

---

[51] Liam Murphy and Thomas Nagel, *The Myth of Ownership: Taxes and Justice* (New York: Oxford University Press, 2002).

intuitive sense of property that they actually use in their business dealings. Any intuitions about property that we bring to
the Rule of Law have to be, in this way, reasonable and flexible
intuitions.

Apart from anything else, what our property amounts
to – certainly what we can do with it – is going to depend
on what else is permitted, what else is prohibited, what else
is regulated in the law at large. Law works holistically. And
property rights are not defined in isolation from the rest of
the law. What my property rights amount to is partly a matter of how things stand in other areas of law. Robert Nozick
once observed that "[m]y property rights in my knife allow
me to leave it where I will, but not in your chest."[52] Property
rights live in the shadow of the criminal law. And it will not
do to turn the tables and say that property rights constrain
the development of the criminal law and place limits on what
uses of material goods the legislature may criminalize. (As in:
"I thought this was *my* gun or *my* marijuana. Why can't I do
with it what I please?")

***

Indeed, I have even heard the argument pushed the other way.
If the Rule of Law protects the expectations we associate with
our property, then the Rule of Law may condemn even the
repeal of some criminal law or regulation if that has an adverse
effect on the value of people's property. Innumerable small
businesses in New York state thrive as liquor stores because
supermarkets are prohibited from selling wine or spirits. Any
proposal to lift the prohibition on supermarket sales would

---

[52] Nozick, *Anarchy, State, and Utopia*, p. 171.

likely encounter howls of outrage from liquor store owners to the effect that this was a way of undermining their private property because it ruined the business plan on which their acquisition of this property was predicated. But we can't have that. We can't have the Rule of Law endorsing a fanatic stabilization which underwrites every expectation of profit that people happen to have conceived in a particular legal context. The Rule of Law is not affronted every time a change in the law upsets people's business plans.

Or consider another example. If someone invests in real estate in upstate New York where a prison is located, anticipating profits from selling homes to corrections officers, they cannot complain on the grounds of the Rule of Law when the discriminatory Rockefeller drug laws are repealed, thus reducing the need for prison spaces to the detriment of their investments. Yet I have heard just such outrage expressed in New York state politics. Admittedly, some of it takes an allegedly more moderate form, with people saying that the repeal should operate only prospectively, with new offenders. They say the changes should not be applied to those currently in the law enforcement pipeline, let alone to those already incarcerated. They say this, not (as critics of retroactivity usually do) in the interest of those subject to the law, but in the interests of the investor expectations they themselves have established. In a spirit of "moderation," the upstate developers acknowledge that the Rule of Law mustn't be construed as prohibiting all changes that affect property, but it does require such change to be measured and slow, rather than abrupt. That way, there will be time for a soft landing for property prices in the prison cities most likely to be affected. Well, moderate or not, it seems to me that we can't have a notion of the Rule of Law that holds public policy hostage to anything remotely like this kind of calculation.[53]

People may say that, without some stability along these lines, you can't have a market in real estate. Take, for example, Mr. Lucas. He bought his beachfront property on the Isle of Palms for development and he wouldn't have paid a penny for it if he hadn't had that possibility – underwritten by traditional doctrines of property – in mind.

But we should be very careful with this point. It is true that you can't have a market in any good or commodity, including land, without a clear sense of who is entitled to sell a piece of land – who is, at the moment of any given transaction, its owner. That has to be determinate and we have to have clear rules for the passage of a given item from one person's ownership to another. Otherwise, market economy is impossible.[54] But it by no means follows that the law has to preserve the value of any given item of property, in order to facilitate market transactions. Indeed, that would more or less make a nonsense of the very idea of a market, where prices are established as a result of hundreds of thousands of transactions and are not under anyone's control. The Rule of Law cannot possibly be cited as a ground for stabilizing prices – certainly not under the auspices of a conception that privileges free

[53] For a good discussion, see Peter A. Mancuso, "Resentencing after the 'Fall' of Rockefeller: The Failure of the Drug Law Reform Acts of 2004 and 2005 to Remedy the Injustices of New York's Rockefeller Drug Laws and the Compromise of 2009," *Albany Law Review* 73 (2010), 1535.
[54] See James Buchanan, *The Limits of Liberty: Between Anarchy and Leviathan* (Chicago: University of Chicago Press, 1975), pp. 17–19.

markets! If uncertainty is the issue, then markets can monet-ize uncertainty. And the monetization of uncertainty can be as sensitive to probabilities concerning legal change as they are to probabilities concerning cyclical economic change. I know this is heresy. A lot of people want a connection between pri-vate property and the Rule of Law that can stand as a major plank in state-building so that foreign investors can have some advance assurance of the amount of wealth they can extract from a developing economy. But no such certainty is available in any other realm of economic activity, and honest jurists working with the notion of the Rule of Law should have noth-ing to do with cynical uses of the ideal that are designed to do nothing more than underwrite the investor-profits of preda-tory and extractive enterprises.

***

We have been considering the shape and the detail of the property rights that might be privileged if property rights were privileged as a substantive dimension of the Rule of Law. It's a difficult subject to say anything about, because – as I said – it is not clear how exactly we are supposed to argue for or against the recognition of private property as a substantive dimension of legality.

But here is an important point to remember. I don't think we can answer the question simply by pointing to the incidents of property that are most important for the individ-uals who have them or to the incidents that are most import-ant for the social functions that private property is supposed to perform or for its role in a market economy. We can't just identify the important incidents of property (in any of these regards) and say that *these* must be the incidents of property that the Rule of Law supports. We can't just say, "Private property is important in this regard and that is why the Rule of Law supports it." If the protection of property is a substantive dimension of the Rule of Law, then presumably it is attuned to property's significance for legality, not to property's significance in itself or in light of other political ideals.

What I mean is that, if the Rule of Law protects private property, it will do so presumably on the Rule of Law's own terms and these may or may not be the terms on which, in other contexts, the principle of private property is extolled. As a thought experiment, imagine someone citing the Rule of Law to resist the abolition of the doctrine of primogeniture. Even if such a person is right in thinking that the Rule of Law privileges private property, he can't assume that it privileges this feature of one traditional conception of private property; on the contrary, the Rule of Law may argue for the abolition of primogeniture in the hope that property will be more widespread and more people will value private property rights accordingly.

As a value in and of itself, private property commands respect in a number of different dimensions of ethical, social, political, and economic importance. But, as a value protected specifically under the auspices of the Rule of Law, it will be protected in those aspects in which values that are already firmly associated with the Rule of Law map on to it. And there's the difficulty: we may have an intuitively plausible or politically convenient association between the Rule of Law and private property, but we have no full or widely accepted explication of why the Rule of Law has this (particular) substantive dimension.

For my money, all this argues in favor of what I called in Chapter 1 the separation thesis.[55] We are better off arguing for the Rule of Law in the respects in which the Rule of Law's concerns cannot be duplicated under the auspices of any other political ideal. And we are better off arguing directly for (or about or against) private property, market economy, and economic freedom in general on the terms that seem most appropriate to those considerations. Arguing in Rule-of-Law terms for property, markets, and economic freedom is simply too distracting. It bogs us down in debates about substantive conceptions and about the sticks in the bundle that are specially privileged as a matter of legality. And it prevents us saying what we want to say about private property for fear that that will not be something that comes under the auspices of the Rule-of-Law ideal.

It may seem a modest conclusion to separate our ideals in this way. And I don't mean that we should be afraid to explore various connections between them. But there is absolutely no point trying to hijack the goodwill invested in one value to try to map it on to another. If we do try that, we may find that all the value leaks out in the process and we end up discrediting the Rule of Law – in every respect – instead of making the case that we want to make about economic freedom.

[55] See the text accompanying Chapter 1, note 20, above.

3

In defense of legislation

The first lecture in this series used the facts of an American case, *Lucas* v. *South Carolina Coastal Council*,[1] to pose a question about the possibility of a special relation between private property and the ideal we call the Rule of Law. The case concerned a property developer, who bought ocean-front real estate intending to develop it as residential property for resale. Unfortunately (or fortunately, depending on your point of view), his plans were thwarted by new environmental regulations intended to protect the coastline from erosion. The developer sued under the Takings Clause of the US Constitution, on the ground that the regulations deprived his property of all or almost all of its value, and his argument was accepted by a majority in the Supreme Court of the United States.

I said that I was not interested in arguing about American constitutional law, but that I wanted to use the facts of *Lucas* v. *South Carolina Coastal Council* to raise a question about the relation between private property and the Rule of Law. Is the property developer's complaint one that can be made in the name of the Rule of Law? Can he proceed with it on the assumption that the Rule of Law should protect his property against this sort of regulation? Or is the ideal of the Rule of Law neutral in this matter, given that there is law on both sides of the equation – law inasmuch as Mr. Lucas's

[1] 505 US 1003 (1992).

76

property rights are legal rights but law also inasmuch as the restriction on development that he faces represents the application of a properly enacted statute?

The Rule of Law, we know, is mainly a formal and procedural ideal. It protects the independence of the judiciary and the proper functioning of the courts; it insists that people should have access to law; and that they should be able to rely upon fair and respectful procedures in the determination of their rights and claims. It insists that the government should operate within a framework of law in everything it does and that it should be challengeable by law and accountable through law when there is a suggestion of wrongful action by those in power. And it insists that governance should take a certain form – that is, that we should be governed on the basis of general laws laid down publicly in advance, operating as a stable and prospective framework to determine people's rights.

In the *Lucas* case, we have property law versus regulatory law. In Chapters 1 and 2, I focused mainly on the property side of the equation. What special position, if any, do property rights have under the Rule of Law? In this chapter, however, I want to turn my attention to the statute which lies in the other tray of the balance. How, in general, should we think about regulative legislation in light of this very important political ideal we have, namely, the ideal of the Rule of Law?

I have written about this elsewhere – but it has been buried in the first issue of the first volume of an obscure journal published out of Belgium, called *Legisprudence*.[2] In that article, I tried to criticize an anti-legislative view that is sometimes

---

[2] See Waldron, "Legislation and the Rule of Law."

associated with the deployment of Rule-of-Law slogans in political economy and in development studies. I wanted to criticize the skepticism about social, economic, and environmental legislation that seems to be characteristic, for example, of the World Bank's approach to the Rule of Law. And that's what I want to pursue in this final chapter.

***

It's a frustrating topic because I don't think this general skepticism is shared these days by most academic or judicial commentators on the Rule of Law. There is no trace of it in Lord Bingham's book, *The Rule of Law*, for example, and I suspect that this skepticism about legislation is not very widely shared among my readers either.

On the contrary, most good-hearted people with an open mind who treasure the idea of the Rule of Law, have very few problems with social, economic, or environmental legislation. If the law is properly drafted (if it is clear and intelligible and expressed in general terms), and it is prospectively enacted and properly promulgated, and if the regulations issued under it are properly made in a way that observes the procedures laid down in the statute and in administrative law generally, and if those regulations are then published and applied subsequently in an impartial way to individual cases without fear or favor according to their terms – if all this is done, then we have an entirely appropriate exercise under the Rule of Law. Indeed, that's what many scholars mean by the Rule of Law: people being governed by measures laid down in advance in general terms and enforced equally according to the terms in which they have been publicly promulgated.

And that is what seems to have happened in the *Lucas* case. There was a series of statutes. A federal law, the Coastal Zone Management Act of 1972, provided a general framework of law and policy for measures of this kind, for the protection of coastlines and beaches from erosion. In 1977, the South Carolina legislature enacted state law under these auspices – making provision for the regulation of coastal areas in the interest of the environment, setting up administrative agencies, and providing a framework for the specification of areas where land was to be zoned and where permits were to be required for development. In 1988, after a blue-ribbon commission found that some of the beaches on the barrier islands were in a critical state, worse than had been feared, South Carolina enacted a further piece of legislation called the Beachfront Management Act. That statute authorized the South Carolina Coastal Council to draw new lines delineating where seaward development would be prohibited or restricted. The council subsequently drew a line in the sand on the landward side of Mr. Lucas's property, in effect prohibiting him from building anything other than a small deck on the land that he owned.[3]

It seems to have been a careful and scrupulous process, both at the various legislative stages and at the administrative stage. True, Mr. Lucas bought his property in 1986, a year or three before the new legislation came into force. But he was not a neophyte in these matters. He was already part of a larger

---

[3] These descriptions are taken from the opinions of the Supreme Court justices in *Lucas*, and also from the opinions of the South Carolina Supreme Court in *Lucas* v. *South Carolina Coastal Council*, 404 SE 2d 895 (1991).

"Wild Dunes" conservation consortium, and like all its members he was almost certainly attuned to the legislature's interest and concerns in this regard. Moreover, the property he purchased in his own name was "notoriously unstable," as Justice Blackmun pointed out in his dissent in the *Lucas* case:

> In roughly half of the last 40 years, all or part of
> Petitioner's property was flooded twice daily by the ebb
> and flow of the tide ... In 1973 the first line of stable
> vegetation was about halfway through the property
> ... Between 1981 and 1983, the Isle of Palms issued 12
> emergency orders for sandbagging to protect property in
> the Wild Dune development ... Determining that local
> habitable structures were in imminent danger of collapse,
> the Council issued permits for two rock revetments to
> protect condominium developments near petitioner's
> property from erosion; one of the revetments extends
> more than halfway onto one of his lots.[4]

In other words, Mr. Lucas was not exactly sand-bagged by the council's eventual intervention to safeguard the eroding beaches on and in the immediate vicinity of his property. (Please note that I am not trying to build a general argument on the basis of any idiosyncrasies of the *Lucas* case; I think rather that Mr. Lucas's position in this regard is typical of those who complain about restrictive legislation. They understand the likelihood of such legislation; but they oppose it, as they are perfectly entitled to do – only sometimes their opposition is expressed disingenuously, on the Rule-of-Law ground that

[4] *Lucas v. South Carolina Coastal Council*, 505 US 1003, pp. 1038–1039 (1992).

they have been taken by surprise by what the legislators have done.)

To me, it seems that in the *Lucas* case, as in many such cases, the whole business was conducted quite lawfully on the legislative side. The legislative purposes were good ones and they are very clearly articulated in the statutes; there were phases of legislative deliberation; there were public commissions; there was the usual notice-and-comment period for agency rule-making; and there is no indication at all that the Coastal Council's determination as to the line that was to be drawn landward of Mr. Lucas's property was anything other than an impartial and reasonable (and, from a procedural point of view, perfectly regular) application of the statute, fully responsive to its articulated concerns.

There is, of course, a very strong current in Rule-of-Law theory that is on the lookout for administrative irregularities and for the statutes that facilitate them by conferring too much untrammeled discretion. That is as it should be, in light of the formal and procedural principles associated with the Rule of Law since Dicey.[5] But that is not the concern here. If the Rule of Law is to take Mr. Lucas's side in the dispute, it has to be on the basis of some objection to legislative intervention as such. It has to be on the basis of a view that there is some affront to the Rule of Law in the very idea of enacting a statute that has this sort of impact on property rights. No matter how scrupulously the statute is drafted, the position we have to contend with is that there is some direct and substantial

[5] See Dicey, *Introduction to the Study of the Law of the Constitution*, pp. lv–lxi.

affront to the Rule of Law in the exercise of this sort of legislative power.

How can that be? As I said, for many of us, the enactment and administration of a properly drafted statute is the essence of the Rule of Law. It is precisely the sort of activity to which (for example) Lon Fuller's famous eight principles of the Rule of Law – the inner morality of law – are properly directed. Generality, clarity, constancy, publicity, prospectivity, and practicability – these are in fact all best understood as virtues of legislation. Indeed, Fuller's presentation of those principles in his *The Morality of Law* was precisely as a discipline incumbent on a legislator, Fuller's rather hapless character, King Rex.[6]

***

Is there anything in Fuller's conception, or the way it has been developed by people like Raz, Finnis, and Bingham, that might explain the uneasiness over legislation? Well, if we stick within the framework of formal and procedural principles, two considerations may give us pause.

First, legislation is something that can be enacted quickly and easily within most legal systems, and as such it may be at odds with the stability that Fuller's principles command and the predictability that the Rule of Law is supposed to promote. South Carolina enacted one statute in 1977 and amended it in 1988, when a public commission determined that the Coastal Council needed greater powers in light of the perceived urgency of the problem. Is that an affront to stability? Is that an excessively destabilizing change in the law?

---

[6] Fuller, *The Morality of Law*, pp. 33–38.

82

I doubt whether many of us, familiar with the cycles of public and legislative attention, would judge it so. But I will talk more about these rhythms and cycles towards the end of this chapter.

Here is a second possibility: Mr. Lucas bought his property in the period intervening between the two pieces of South Carolina's legislation. The first statute was enacted in 1977, and its planning ramifications were clear by the time Mr. Lucas bought his two residential lots in 1986. But the second piece of legislation, enacted in 1988, applied to all property on the ocean front including his. Does that mean there was an objectionable element of retroactivity?

It has sometimes been said that the Takings Clause works in tandem with the *ex post facto* clause in Article One of the US Constitution so that between them they cover all forms of retroactivity. But I don't think the *Lucas* case involves retroactivity, any more than I think that a statute changing the speeding fines is retrospective with regard to my operation of an automobile I purchased several years ago. Certainly Mr. Lucas had not commenced any development work on his property before the second statute was passed. Had work commenced before the statute was passed and had that work been declared unlawful, then we would have had a clear case of retroactivity. But that was not what happened.

I said earlier that Mr. Lucas knew perfectly well that the legislation on beach erosion was in flux, and that it was quite likely that property such as his might be affected. I don't quite want to get into the position that some courts have reached, where they have indicated that public dissatisfaction with a law or attention to the trajectory of law reform or law reform in adjacent states can substitute for the formal notice associated with the actual passage and promulgation of a stat- ute.[7] I don't want to go down that road. Retroactivity is not cured by prior notice of an intention to change the law.

Still, I think it is inappropriate to apply the principle prohibiting retroactive legislation to statutes that affect the use of land purchased or inherited before the statute was passed. Though some property circulates quickly, almost as a commodity, other land remains in the stable possession of a single owner or a single family for generations, and it would be quite wrong to insist that the legal situation with regard to the use of that land must remain stable and unchanged throughout that period. Much better to say that one who comes into possession of a piece of land necessarily is aware that what he can do with it will be changed and affected by the rhythm of ordinary law-making from time to time. People know that there are such things as environmental concerns – particularly people in Mr. Lucas's position. They know that those concerns are seen as urgent and compelling and that they evolve over time, both in their underlying principles and in terms of environmental strategy. This should come as no surprise. It is part of general civic responsibility to be alert to these matters and to adjust one's expectations accordingly so far as those concern what one can do with one's property.

***

So if it is not the retroactivity of the impact or the frequency of the enactments, what *is* the concern about legislation?

---

[7] See e.g. *Rogers* v. *Tennessee*, 532 US 451 (2001), in which a criminal defendant was deemed to have had notice of a change in the Common Law's "year-and-a-day" rule in Tennessee by virtue of public dissatisfaction with it and its gradual abolition in other states.

No one doubts that a statute can undermine the Rule of Law. If you want an example, you can look at the statute enacted in New Zealand in the wake of the first Christchurch earthquake in 2010 that provided (among other things) that the Crown could suspend the operation of any statute – apart from a dozen or so that were listed, including the New Zealand Bill of Rights Act – if that statute threatened to "divert resources away from the effort to efficiently respond to the damage caused by the Canterbury earthquake."[8] And we are all sickeningly familiar with occasional attempts by legislators to remove legal remedies, obstruct the operation of the courts, or preclude judicial review of executive action.[9] But this is not legislation as such; this is a concern about the content of particular enactments. So let's see if we can get a feel for this broader discomfort – the sort of discomfort you find in Hayek's later work, for example[10] – at the level of general jurisprudence.

---

[8] Canterbury Earthquake Response and Recovery Act 2010, section 6.

[9] The classic discussion of this is in *Anisminic Ltd* v. *Foreign Compensation Commission* [1969] 2 AC 147. Consider also section 950(j)(b) of the Military Commissions Act 2006 (10 USC 950a) in the United States, enacted in the wake of *Hamdan* v. *Rumsfeld*, 548 US 557 (2006), providing that "no court, justice, or judge shall have jurisdiction to hear or consider any claim or cause of action whatsoever, including any action pending on or filed after the date of the enactment of the Military Commissions Act of 2006, relating to the prosecution, trial, or judgment of a military commission under this chapter, including challenges to the lawfulness of procedures of military commissions under this chapter."

[10] Discomfort about legislation as such is most clearly expressed in Hayek's later work, where he draws a pretty sharp contrast between the concept of law and the concept of legislation, and suggests that the Rule

I suspect it is a concern about voluntarism, the role of human will and agency in a legal system. Legislation is a matter of *will* – so much a matter of will that it seems ill-suited for celebration under the auspices of a political ideal whose purpose many understand to be the taming or reduction of the role played by will in politics. The legislative process produces law simply by virtue of a bunch of politicians *deciding* that law is to be produced. As I said in *The Dignity of Legislation*, there does seem to be something brazen about this: "We have decided that this will be the law; so it is the law. And what the law is from now on is exactly the content of our decision."[11] And this is said by the very men – powerful politicians – to whose rule the Rule of Law is supposed to be an alternative.

Admittedly, this apprehension about sheer voluntarism under the cloak of law can be applied to other legal sources as well. There are similar apprehensions about activist judges who understand their own power in purely decisionist

of Law comes close to meaning the opposite of the rule of legislation. Hayek in his later work contrasts law with legislation, and suggests that the Rule of Law comes close to meaning the opposite of the rule of legislation. See Hayek, *Rules and Order*, pp. 72–73 and 124–144. In Hayek's earlier discussions of the Rule of Law, this is discernible (just), but it is very muted: see e.g. *The Constitution of Liberty*, p. 157: "Most of these rules have never been deliberately invented but have grown through a gradual process of trial and error in which the experience of successive generations has helped to make them what they are." Mostly, the conception of the Rule of Law presented in *The Constitution of Liberty* could be applied quite naturally to legislation, whereas the later work, *Rules and Order*, evinces great hostility towards legislation and legislatures.

[11]   See Waldron, *The Dignity of Legislation*, pp. 12 and 24.

terms.[12] Rule by judges, also, is sometimes seen as the very sort of rule by men that the Rule of Law is supposed to supersede.[13] When Justice Stevens of the US Supreme Court wrote, in his dissent in *Bush* v. *Gore*,[14] that the true loser in that case was the Rule of Law, he meant precisely to contrast that ideal with a decision of a willful and politically motivated (or at best lawlessly and pragmatically motivated) majority of his brethren on the bench.[15] But, although this cynicism about the law can be turned in this way against judicial law-making, it is more common (and more easily available to lazy minds) as turned against legislation.

Yet another way of capturing the same uneasiness, underlying this hostility towards legislation, is to think about

[12] See e.g. the concern of Herbert Wechsler in "Toward Neutral Principles of Constitutional Law," *Harvard Law Review* 73 (1959), 1, pp. 10–11: "Are there, indeed, any criteria that both the Supreme Court and those who undertake to praise or to condemn its judgments are morally and intellectually obligated to support? Those who perceive in law only the element of fiat, in whose conception of the legal cosmos reason has no meaning or no place, will not join gladly in the search for standards of the kind I have in mind."

[13] See the discussion in Waldron, "Is the Rule of Law an Essentially Contested Concept (in Florida)?," pp. 142–143 and 147–148.

[14] 531 US 98 (2000).

[15] *Bush* v. *Gore*, 531 US 98, pp. 128–129 (Stevens J., dissenting): "It is confidence in the men and women who administer the judicial system that is the true backbone of the Rule of Law. Time will one day heal the wound to that confidence that will be inflicted by today's decision. One thing, however, is certain. Although we may never know with complete certainty the identity of the winner of this year's Presidential election, the identity of the loser is perfectly clear. It is the Nation's confidence in the judge as an impartial guardian of the Rule of Law."

the relation between legislation and the state. The Rule of Law is commonly seen as a way of limiting the power of the state, keeping the power of the state under control. But legislation is normally understood as one of the most important aspects of the power of the modern state. It is not the sole mode of state action, but, with regard to the more important policies of the state, it is often an indispensable step in policy implementation. What legislation does is mobilize governmental and administrative resources for the achievement of governmental aims: when the state needs something done, legislation is usually the first step in the doing of it.[16] It is something the state controls and manipulates as a tool for its own purposes. But, it is said – and this again is a common theme in connection with the issues we are considering – the value we place in the Rule of Law is not in the rule of state law. Instead, what we want is a Rule-of-Law state, and that is something quite different.[17]

So, if legislation is viewed just as a governmental directive, then – these people will say – maybe it *is* a mistake to regard enforcement of and compliance with such directives as signifying anything very important in relation to the Rule of Law. Enforcement of, and compliance with, legislation would be a measure of how powerful and effective the state is, and how well organized its apparatus is. But it would not tell us

---

[16] See Edward Rubin, "Law and Legislation in the Administrative State," *Columbia Law Review* 89 (1989), 369, pp. 372–373.

[17] Robert Cooter, "The Rule of State Law versus the Rule-of-Law State: Economic Analysis of the Legal Foundations of Development," in E. Buscaglia, W. Ratliff, and R. Cooter, *The Law and Economics of Development* (Greenwich, CT: JAI Press, 1997), p. 101.

much about controls on that apparatus, and that is mostly what we want to know under the heading of "the Rule of Law."

I mentioned a little while ago F. A. Hayek's antipathy to legislation, his suggestion that rule by legislation represents almost the opposite of the Rule of Law.[18] According to Hayek, the legislative mentality is inherently managerial; it is oriented in the first instance to the organization of the state's administrative apparatus; and its extension into the realm of public policy generally means an outward projection of that sort of managerial mentality with frightful consequences for liberty and markets. And that, says Hayek, is the very thing the Rule of Law is supposed to oppose. The Rule of Law, he says, refers to something different – an order of impersonal norms that emerge and evolve, more like Common Law,[19] rather than norms that are posited and manufactured and come bearing legislators' names like the McCain–Feingold Act.[20] Legislation may occasionally be necessary if law's implicit development has led us into some sort of *cul-de-sac*, but this acknowledgment by Hayek is grudging;[21] it is a reluctant recognition that this kind of law-making may sometimes be necessary

---

[18] Hayek, *Rules and Order*, pp. 72–73 and 124–144.

[19] Needless to say, in this celebration, the Rule-of-Law difficulties of the Common Law are conveniently forgotten: its opacity, the *ad hoc* character of its development, its unpredictability, and its inherent retroactivity. For good accounts, see Jeremy Bentham, *Of Laws in General*, ed. H. L. A. Hart (London: Athlone Press, 1970), pp. 184–195; and Gerald Postema, *Bentham and the Common Law Tradition* (Oxford: Oxford University Press, 1986), pp. 267–301.

[20] Bipartisan Campaign Reform Act of 2002.

[21] Hayek, *Rules and Order*, pp. 88–89.

(as something compromising the Rule of Law) rather than a recognition of legislation's place in that ideal.

***

I mentioned in Chapter 1 the use of Rule-of-Law indexes to rate countries for the benefit of investors and others seeking to do business in a particular legal or commercial environment. On these indexes, the extent of a society's adherence to the Rule of Law is not determined (or determined only in very small part) by the effectiveness of its enforcement of existing legislation (or its capacity to enforce future legislation). Many of the measures these indexes for the Rule of Law could have been used in the time of Adam Smith, without regard to the rise of the modern legislative and regulatory state and the concerns that underlie it.[22]

Indeed, it is often implied that a society's score on a Rule-of-Law index may be diminished by the effective enforcement of legislation if the tendency of such legislation is to interfere with market processes or to limit property rights

[22] According to James Wolfensohn, when he was President of the World Bank, the Rule of Law means that: "A government must ensure that it has an effective system of property, contracts, labor, bankruptcy, commercial codes, personal rights law and other elements of a comprehensive legal system that are effectively, impartially, and cleanly administered by a well-functioning, impartial and honest judicial and legal system." Wolfensohn, as quoted by Frank Upham, "Mythmaking in the Rule of Law Orthodoxy," Carnegie Endowment Working Paper No. 30 (Washington, DC: Carnegie Endowment for International Peace, 2002). What is missing in this account? Well, compliance by business, industry, and commerce with legal regulation of the marketplace and with limitations placed on the use of property (e.g. for environmental reasons). Compliance with legislation, the enforcement of regulations – these aspects of the Rule of Law are deafening in their silence here.

or to make investment in the society more precarious or in other ways less remunerative to outsiders. The Rule of Law, on this view, requires a government to offer assurances that it will not legislate in this way or that it will keep such legislation to a minimum; it may call for legal and constitutional guarantees for property rights (and perhaps also for other rights) against legislative encroachment; and it may require provision for judicial review, that is, for offending legislation to be struck down by courts.

Those who take this approach acknowledge that some deliberately crafted law is necessary. It is important, for example, that there be a clearly articulated criminal code. (Even those Rule-of-Law theorists who model their ideal on unlegislated private law are not comfortable with the idea of Common Law offenses.) And often, in a developing society, legislation is necessary in order to establish the institutions and procedural frameworks through which law operates, and by which legal rights are protected, and maybe also to establish clear frameworks, procedures, and expectations in the area of corporate law, bankruptcy, and so on.[23] Still, the idea is that we can distinguish between legislation as a framing and facilitating device for the autonomous operation of a well-functioning legal system, and legislation as a medium through which regulatory or public policy goals are pursued. Legislation of the latter sort *is* inherently subject to suspicion from the point of view of the World Bank approach to the Rule of Law, for it threatens

---

[23] See e.g. K. Pistor in J.D. Sachs and K. Pistor (eds.), *The Rule of Law and Economic Reform in Russia* (Westview, 1997), "Company Law and Corporate Governance in Russia," p. 165.

radically to limit or undermine the property rights, market arrangements, and investment opportunities which the Rule of Law is supposed to frame and guarantee.[24] What people have in mind here is environmental legislation, legislation favorable to labor, restrictions on freedom of contract, restrictions on investment or on profit-taking, legislation nationalizing assets or industries, price restrictions, and so on.

The view we are considering is one element in a more general approach to economy and development, associated with what is sometimes called the Washington Consensus.[25] On this account, the whole point of the Rule of Law is the promotion of market institutions and the establishment of an atmosphere conducive to profitable investment.[26] Concomitantly,

---

[24] For example, see I. Shihata, "Relevant Issues in the Establishment of a Sound Legal Framework for a Market Economy," in I. Shihata, *The World Bank in a Changing World* (Boston: Martinus Nijhoff, 2000), vol. III, p. 187: "An over-regulated economy undermines new investment, increases the costs of existing ones and leads to the spread of corruption. Multiplication of laws and regulations often reduces their quality and the chances of their enforcement. The absence of judicial review, or its high cost … add to the negative impact."

[25] See e.g. J. Williamson, "Democracy and the 'Washington Consensus,'" *World Development* 21 (1993), 1329; and J. M. Ngugi, "Policing Neo-Liberal Reforms: The Rule of Law as an Enabling and Restrictive Discourse," *University of Pennsylvania Journal of International Economic Law* 26 (2005), 513, p. 599.

[26] The literature is very extensive. For examples, see: Thomas Carothers, "The Rule of Law Revival," *Foreign Affairs* 77 (1998), 95; Barro, "Determinants of Democracy"; I. Shihata, "The World Bank and 'Governance' Issues in Its Borrowing Members," in F. Tschofen and A. Parra (eds.), *The World Bank in a Changing World: Selected Essays* (Boston: Martinus Nijhoff, 1991), p. 53; and I. Shihata, "Legal Framework

the thought is that we need to keep legislation and the pro-
pensity to legislate under very firm control. And it would be
good (these people go onto say) if that control could be exercised under the auspices of the Rule of Law – an ideal that is
so popular, conveys so many good vibrations, and commands
such support across the political spectrum. You don't find a
lot of this in academic writing about the Rule of Law, but, as
I have said, you will see it in journals of political economy, or
in World Bank literature, or in development studies.

**

The view we are considering – the approach that denigrates
legislation in the name of the Rule of Law – is often expressed
in this literature as a view about democratization. Those who
espouse the view I am considering may concede grudgingly
that societies have a legitimate aspiration to govern themselves. They may accept that a modern society does need
eventually to set up and operate a representative legislature.
They will recognize this as part of the normal aspiration to
democracy. But it would be good, some of them say, especially in the early stages of nation-building, if such institutions could be confined to playing a marginal role in the
governance of the society, for fear that they will undermine
the development or marketization of the country's economy.[27] In Chapter 1, I mentioned the work of Robert Barro,
a political economist at Harvard, who believes that the main
value of Rule-of-Law indexes is to provide information on

for Development," in *The World Bank in a Changing World* (Boston:
Martinus Nijhoff, 1995), vol. II, p. 127.
[27] For discussion, see Thomas Carothers, "Rule of Law Temptations,"
Fletcher Forum 33 (2009), 49.

country risk to foreign investors. Barro also believes that the empirical evidence supports the assertion that "democracy is a moderate deterrent to the maintenance of the rule of law."[28] In his view, this suggests an order of developmental priorities: democratization should take second place to legalization in nation-building.[29] And, if legalization – the building of Rule of Law – has priority over democracy, then it must also have priority over legislation which is the work-product of democracy. That is why, on Barro's view, we are compelled to signal this priority with a conception of the Rule of Law that distinguishes it from the enactment and enforcement of statutes.

***

What should we say about all this? As you would expect from someone who authored a book called *The Dignity of Legislation*, I have very little patience with this view. To my mind, it is very odd that the effective operation of a legislature should be separated in this way from the Rule of Law. And now, having described the view that I want to criticize, I am going to go over onto the offensive (though in a way that

---

[28] Robert Barro, *Getting It Right: Markets and Choices in a Free Society* (Cambridge, MA: MIT Press, 1996), p. 7. He continues: "This result is not surprising because more democracy means that the political process allows the majority to extract resources legally from minorities (or powerful interest groups to extract resources legally from the disorganized majority)."

[29] *Ibid.*, p. 11: "[T]he advanced Western countries would contribute more to the welfare of poor nations by exporting their economic systems, notably property rights and free markets, rather than their political systems, which typically developed after reasonable standards of living had been attained."

requires us to step back for a moment and to consider the general topic of legal change).

We know that, in any legal system, legislation is not the only source of law, not the only source of legal change. Law also comes into existence and changes in a society through the decisions of courts, through executive rule-making, and through the signing and ratification of treaties. But the legislature occupies a pre-eminent role in most legal systems, largely due to the fact that it is an institution set up explicitly – dedicated explicitly – to the making and changing of the law.[30] Though the law-making role of the courts is well known to legal professionals, judicial decision-making does not present itself in public as a process for changing or creating law. Judges constantly assure the public – disingenuously, we (insiders) know, but constantly – that their role is to find the law, not make it. Law-making by courts is not a transparent process; law-making in a legislature, by contrast, is law-making through a procedure dedicated publicly and transparently to that task. This ought to matter. One of the most important things about the Rule-of-Law ideal is its emphasis on transparency in governance, and one would think that that would be important in the present context as well.

Not only that, but one would think that, if the Rule of Law requires that law be taken seriously and held in high regard in a society, then particular emphasis should be given

---

[30] See also Jeremy Waldron, "Principles of Legislation," in Richard Bauman and Tsvi Kahana (eds.), *The Least Examined Branch: The Role of Legislatures in the Constitutional State* (Cambridge: Cambridge University Press, 2006), pp. 15 and 22–23.

THE RULE OF LAW

to the legitimacy of the processes by which legislatures enact statutes. Again, think of the contrast with courts. Not only do judges pretend diffidently that they are just finding not making the law, we know also that any widespread impression among members of the public that judges were acting as law-makers would seriously detract from the legitimacy of their decisions.

And this popular perception is not groundless. Courts are not set up in a way that is calculated to make law-making legitimate. Legislatures, by contrast, are organized – and occasionally reformed and rehabilitated – explicitly to make their law-making activity legitimate. If we think that the operation of the electoral system has led to some section of the community being wrongly disenfranchised so far as legislative representation is concerned, then that will be widely regarded as a reason for reforming a legislature and its election procedures. (It may not happen as often as it ought to, but it is still recognized as a good reason for reform.) We want our laws to be made in an institution that properly represents us all. In this and other ways we pay constant attention to the issue of the legitimacy of the legislature as a law-maker; and, by doing this, we ensure that there is something to be said to a citizen who opposes a new law why it is fair nevertheless to require him to submit to it. We pay attention to the legitimacy of courts, too, but not to their legitimacy *as law-makers*; instead, we look at issues like fairness *inter partes*, and to issues about procedure and delay, and perhaps also to the substantive rationality of decisions. But, since we know that the law-making of courts can bind the whole community on the basis of a decision responsive only to the arguments of two parties, this is a very curious way to go about securing legitimacy for legal change.

In general, legislation has the characteristic that it gives ordinary people a sort of stake in the Rule of Law, by involving them directly or indirectly in its enactment, and by doing so on terms of fair political equality. I mentioned earlier de Tocqueville's early observation on legality in America: if you want to instill respect for law, he said, making law through elective processes is one of the best ways to do it.[31] Of course, every law will have its opponents, those whose representatives were outvoted in the relevant session of the legislature. Still, as de Tocqueville said, "in the United States everyone is personally interested in enforcing the obedience of the whole community to the law; for as the minority may shortly rally the majority to its principles, it is interested in professing that respect for the decrees of the legislator which it may soon have occasion to claim for its own."[32] But, if legislation is denigrated as a source of law for the purposes of the Rule-of-Law ideal, then it is not at all clear where respect for the law, which the Rule of Law requires, is supposed to come from.

***

I spoke earlier about voluntarism. Objections to legislation that rest on the perception of some sort of wholesale incompatibility between legislation and the Rule of Law tend to make the element of human *agency* pivotal. Legislation is the political construction of law – intentionally and explicitly. Those who feel this discomfort want the Rule of Law to

---

[31] De Tocqueville, *Democracy in America*, pp. 244–248 (vol. I, Chapter 14). See the text accompanying Chapter 1, note 21, above.
[32] *Ibid.*, p. 247.

find and accredit modes of legality that manage somehow to eschew political agency, because they think that any concession to human agency undermines the celebrated distinction between the rule of law and the rule of man. And so they look to the Common Law as an emergent evolving body of law and they look to markets in which property rights circulate autonomously without political intervention.

Of course, there is agency in a property market. But it is not the agency of politicians inventing and imposing a particular vision of how things should be distributed. There is only the agency of hundreds of thousands of individuals working through a given legal framework – as buyers and sellers, landlords and tenants, mortgagors and mortgagees, stock-holders and managers. And this agency of individuals is not supposed to pose a problem, because it is exactly the kind of thing that the elimination of political agency is supposed to make room for. It is slightly harder to make the case that the Common Law operates apolitically. After all, judges are political officials – in a sense – and the law at any time is the resultant of hundreds of judge-made decisions. But, again, it is thought that the case-by-case incremental nature of this decision-making avoids the imperious and comprehensive visions that legislators aspire to and that they seek, by their human rule, to impose.

Myself – I am skeptical about the very idea of eschewing human agency in our conception of the Rule of Law. The Rule of Law is about law and governance and it is necessarily oriented to what is done – to what people do – in the way of governing themselves or each other. We fantasize sometimes about a society being ordered acephalously,[33] without deliberation or deliberate decision, being ruled (as it were) directly by morality or by immemorial traditions and mores that no one has responsibility for. Morality, as H. L. A. Hart reminded us, is immune from deliberate change.[34] This is as true of the embedded positive morality of a society as it is of the real moral reasons, values, and principles that constitute what Hart called critical morality or that we might call morality *tout court*. Positive mores may change gradually but not as a result of deliberation or deliberate human agency. The introduction of law, by contrast, is the deliberate introduction of the possibility that changes may be made in the way that a society is ordered. That's part of what law means, on Hart's account; the union of primary rules of conduct, which may once have been immemorial, with secondary rules that empower a society to take responsibility for the primary order, adapt it flexibly to changing social conditions, and keep track of and monitor the changes that stand in the name of us all through a rule of recognition.[35] That's what law essentially is, and the principle we call the Rule of Law can't in its essence be antagonistic to

[33] See e.g. on the state of nature, Locke, *Two Treatises of Government*, pp. 288–289, 348, and 368–370 (Book II, Chapter II, § 6, Chapter VIII, § 95, and Chapter IX, §§ 123–128). For real world examples, see Michael Taylor, *Community, Anarchy and Liberty* (Cambridge: Cambridge University Press, 1982).

[34] Hart, *The Concept of Law*, pp. 175–178.

[35] *Ibid.*, pp. 95–96. For the primacy of rules of change in Hart's account, see Jeremy Waldron, "Who Needs Rules of Recognition?," in Matthew Adler and Kenneth Einar Himma (eds.), *The Rule of Recognition and the US Constitution* (Oxford: Oxford University Press, 2009), p. 327.

that. It is essential to law that it be susceptible to deliberate change, and, though the Rule-of-Law ideal may patrol that and discipline it, it cannot be understood as an ideal designed to preclude such change.

Hayek says that this emphasis on change is already infected by a positivist mentality – no wonder that it was sponsored as an essential element of law by the arch-modern positivist, H. L. A. Hart. But, Hayek reminds us, positivism is just one option in jurisprudence, and he thinks for various reasons (some of them good, some of them bad) that it is a discredited option.[36] But do things really look any different if jurisprudence swings to an anti-positivist point of view? It may seem so. The rule of natural law seems a wonderful paradigm of legal stability – a timeless and objective law, built into nature or the real moral structure of the world, or the enduring commands of an eternally faithful God. It doesn't change, and certainly we cannot change it. As John Finnis puts it in *Natural Law and Natural Rights*, "of natural law itself there could be strictly speaking no history."[37]

But appearances are deceptive, and this inference of stability from a hypothesis of natural law is a mistake, for two connected reasons. First, if circumstances are changing, then the ultimate deliverances of natural law (so far as concerns, for example, who has what natural property rights) will change too: a constant set of principles applied to changing circumstances (where the principle is formulated in a way that is sensitive to the relevant circumstances) will lead to changing

[36] Hayek, *Rules and Order*, p. 73.
[37] Finnis, *Natural Law and Natural Rights*, p. 24.

results. When population changes drastically, expanding (say) from the thousands to the millions; or when climate changes with inundation or desertification, bringing new and unprecedented dilemmas of resource use, then the application of constant principles will not yield constant results.

Anyway, second, even if natural law has no history, our understanding of natural law has a history – we may have got it wrong (in principle or in application) in the past, and now we have to change what we say it implies, our sense of what it implies, to reflect the repudiation of our errors. Natural law was once thought by some people to sanction slavery or the subordination of women; now we know better. Our sense of natural law has a history, even if the abstract principles laid up in heaven (which have sometimes managed to elude our understanding) are themselves timeless in character. So any human legal system that purports to be based on natural law cannot eschew the agency involved in deliberation or deliberate change, for fear of embedding its own errors or for fear of being unresponsive to the varied ways in which constant moral reasons interact with changing circumstances. The point here is not to convince you to take a natural law approach. It is to show that nothing in particular turns on one's jurisprudential choice in this debate between positivism and natural law – on either account, we have to set ourselves up to accept and consecrate flexible law, changeable law, including law changing deliberately through explicit thought and social decision, including, in other words, legislation.

So, when Justice Kennedy said in his concurrence in *Lucas* v. *South Carolina Coastal Council* that "[t]he State should not be prevented from enacting new regulatory initiatives in response to changing conditions" and that "the Takings Clause does not require a static body of state property law," that is as true on a natural law approach as it is on a positivist approach.

* * *

Some will say that, even if all this is true of law in general, there is nevertheless a case to be made for slowing down the pace of change and minimizing the impact of change on rights of private property and the operation of free markets, for it is in these areas that security of expectation is particularly important and the confidence of proprietors and investors must particularly be paid attention to. Ronald Cass, who has written extensively about the relationship between the Rule of Law and private property, takes this view. On the one hand, Cass concedes that "[t]here is no way to bar change in the law or to make property rights absolutely secure against such change."[38] Change, he says, "is a natural part of any legal system, and efforts to limit change must be seen not as ends in themselves but as part of a larger framework for assuring predictable, valid, law-based governance."[39] But still, he insists, "[t]he ways in which systems manage changes in property rights and in legal rules that affect property rights ... are the keys to the effectiveness of the rule of law,"[40] and he insists that this must be particularly so in the case of land reform.

I addressed this theme of the stability of property that is required for market economy in Chapter 2. In that chapter,

---

[38] Ronald A. Cass, "Property Rights Systems and the Rule of Law," Boston University School of Law Working Paper Series, Public Law and Legal Theory No. 03-06, available at http://ssrn.com/abstract=392783.

[39] *Ibid.*, p. 2.   [40] *Ibid.*

I acknowledged the point that you can't have a market in any good or commodity, including land, without a clear sense of who is entitled to sell a piece of land – who is, at the moment of any given transaction, its owner. That has to be determinate, and we have to have clear rules for the passage of a given item from one person's ownership to another. Otherwise, markets are impossible. But I said that it doesn't follow that law has to protect the value of any given item of property, in order to facilitate market transactions. A case can perhaps be made that the establishment and protection of property rights is one of the paradigmatic functions of law: this function for law responds to some of the most elementary circumstances of the human condition such as our need for resources, our limited altruism, and the need to mitigate what David Hume called "the easy transition from one person to another … of the enjoyment of such possessions as we have acquir'd by our industry and good fortune."[41] It is part of what H. L. A. Hart called "the minimum content of natural law."[42] All this we can grant.

But it is inevitable in the world we live in that the nature and legitimacy of property rights will be affected over time by changes in circumstances, both in their character and in their distribution. The exploitation of land and other natural resources in a way that ignores public goods or the prospect of great public evils is not always tolerable. And the pace of our recognition of this is going to have to accelerate in breadth and

---

[41] Hume, *A Treatise of Human Nature*, pp. 487–489. I have reversed the order of two quotations here, without altering the sense.
[42] Hart, *The Concept of Law*, pp. 193–200.

intensity over the next fifty years if decent conditions of life are to have any chance of surviving the man-made changes in climate that are presently beginning to affect us.

Likewise, extreme and growing inequalities are not always tolerable. The basis on which private property rights were initially allocated may turn out to be inequitable in light of changing circumstances or they may always have been inequitable, and market circulation may have done nothing to reduce that inequity. For example, the transition that many societies in Eastern and Central Europe and the former Soviet Union have undergone from collective property arrangements to a private property economy is one that needs careful and continuing management and scrutiny, for the first steps that were taken have not always proved to be the steps that the society can be expected to live with in perpetuity. They may generate oligarchies and under-classes – entrenched structures of arrogance and resentment that are at odds with the basis of a decent social order. The broad social consequences of privatization in various areas are not always easy to foresee. Eventually, inequalities become intolerable.

And, thirdly, what markets can and cannot produce, and how efficient they are at producing it (or what social goals they promote or retard in various circumstances) are not always calculable *a priori*. This too varies over time and with circumstances in the face of social, economic, ecological, and demographic change. The circumstances vary and – as I said in my comments on natural law – our apprehension of the relevant principles and circumstances can vary too, with the state of our knowledge and the state of our politics. So we may need to adjust either the framework of markets or the reach of markets in various ways. No sensible person, I think, can doubt this after 2008.

That matters like these may need collective attention from time to time is not a cranky or anomalous position; it is not Bolshevik or socially destructive; *it is the ordinary wisdom of human affairs*. No conception of governance, no conception of law that fails to leave room for changes and adjustments of this sort can possibly be tolerable. And it seems to me that any conception of the Rule of Law which denigrates the very idea of such changes and which treats their enforcement as an inherent derogation from that ideal has to be wrong.

Any particular proposal for change will no doubt have its opponents, and sometimes or often the opponents will be right. They may be right because a proposed environmental regulation proves unnecessary or hysterical, or because a given piece of social legislation represents nothing more than cynical rent-seeking by one faction exploiting another. These are enduring possibilities in the sordid and shabby circumstances of human politics. But the opponents are not necessarily right all the time or even right as often as not. It is a matter of judgment, social and political, and one to be made by the people of the country concerned, through active political debate, as they consider the need for change, the proposals for change, and the costs as well as the benefits of implementing such proposals.

On the other hand, those who insist that, once markets and property rights have been established, any change or any regulation is out of the question characteristically take the perspective of an outsider, interested only (like the investors that Robert Barro referred to when he talked about the sale and purchase of Rule-of-Law indexes)[43] in what can be extracted from a given society. This is certainly not the perspective of someone who lives in the society and cares about changes in the quality of life (and changes in the distribution of the quality of life among his or her fellow inhabitants) that markets and property rights are supposed to contribute to. Responsiveness to these changes and willingness to express concern about them is the hallmark of the responsible citizen, and we should be wary of adopting any conception of the Rule of Law that is designed to sideline or discredit that. We should be especially wary when such conception is advocated from an external or predatory point of view.

So, changes in the regulation of property and market structures are not necessarily out of order. Of course, everything depends on the mode of such changes. Constant day-to-day managerial meddling or changes imposed by decree are rightly regarded as incompatible with the Rule of Law. But *legislated* changes are not necessarily incompatible with that ideal. On the contrary, not only does an adequate conception of the Rule of Law have to leave room for them; an adequate conception *envisages* such changes inasmuch as it subjects them to formal and procedural criteria of legality. The Rule of Law will insist on changes enacted openly through procedures that are transparent and clear, changes that are formulated prospectively in general terms, changes that take the form of established schemes that people can expect to see upheld and enforced in the medium and long term, changes set out publicly in intelligible legal texts and then given to

---

[43] Barro, "Determinants of Democracy," p. S173.

independent judicial tribunals for interpretation, administration, and enforcement.

I am not making a case for the sort of flexibility that is characterized by peremptory or ill-considered legislation. I am a great believer in legislative due process. Legislating is not the same as the issuing of a decree; it is a formally defined act consisting of a laborious process. In a well-structured legislature, that process involves public consultation and the commissioning of reports and consultative papers; as well as the informal stages of public debate, it includes also successive stages of formal deliberation in the legislature, deliberation and voting in institutional settings where the legislative proposal is subject to scrutiny at the hands of myriad representatives of various social interests.

These procedural virtues – legislative due process, if you like – are of the utmost importance for the Rule of Law. Not nearly enough is written about them.[44] Bicameralism, checks and balances (such as executive veto), the production of a text as the focus of deliberation, clause-by-clause consideration, the formality and solemnity of the treatment of bills in the chamber, the publicity of legislative debates, successive layers of deliberation inside and outside the chamber, and the sheer time for consideration – formal and informal consideration, internal and external to the legislature – that is allowed to pass between the initiation and the final enactment of a bill: these are all features of legislative due process that are salient

---

[44] I have tried to address the topic of legislative due process in Waldron, *Law and Disagreement* (Oxford: Clarendon Press, 1999), Chapter 4; in Waldron, "Legislating with Integrity," *Fordham Law Review* 72 (2003), 373; and in Waldron, "Principles of Legislation."

to an enactment's eventual status as law (for the purposes of our thinking about the Rule of Law).

To wish to be subject to the Rule of Law is to wish to be subject to enactments that have been through processes like these. When we say, for example, that the Rule of Law requires that no one should be punished except pursuant to the violation of some rule that was laid down before he offended – *nulla poena sine lege* – we don't just have in mind an edict or a decree issued in advance. We have in mind that the prohibition which he is accused of violating is one that was enacted in advance through the laborious solemnity of the legislative process, enacted as law not just given out as notice.

True, legislation is sometimes adopted in haste or under urgency; but by and large that is something that should be criticized in the name of the Rule of Law – and in the Rule-of-Law indexes, the score given to countries that allow it as a typical mode of law-making (such as New Zealand, which otherwise has a very high score on the World Bank's Rule-of-Law index) should be marked down sharply for this sort of abuse.[45]

And no doubt these requirements of legislative due process mitigate the pace of legal change, if they are properly observed, and this may go some way to addressing the concerns that property owners have about the security and stability of their expectations. But I don't think it is possible to go

---

[45] See Jeremy Waldron, "Parliamentary Recklessness: Why We Need to Legislate More Carefully," *New Zealand Law Journal* (2008), 458, available also at www.maxim.org.nz/files/pdf/jeremywaldron_parliamentaryrecklessness.pdf.

much further than that. The discipline of the Rule of Law, and in particular the discipline of legislative due process, already imposes substantial constraints on the alacrity with which a society can respond collectively and deliberatively to changing circumstances. We must remember too that the rhythm of change that this imposes needs to be matched with the rhythm of politics, because it is not easy to develop a platform and assemble and sustain a coalition for change all the way through this process. (This is perhaps harder in an American-style legislature, than in the Westminster system, though legislating at Westminster is proving (or will prove) more and more difficult as executive dominance gives way to specifically parliamentary institutionalization of the safeguards of legislative due process. I have in mind the growth of select committees, for example, independent of the executive, and the increasingly assertive power of a changing second chamber.)

But what I don't think we should concede is that the rhythm and timetabling of a society's legislative flexibility should be adjusted additionally to pander to the profit horizons of individual investors who crave a certainty in the property market that they cannot secure in other investment environments.

***

In the bequest that established this series of lectures, Emma Hamlyn stipulated that the lecturer should aim to remind the common people of England of the privilege of living under law. I doubt that the common people need all that much reminding. They are aware of the good that is done by our institutions and legal ideals. We have democratic institutions because we want to maintain equal respect for one another in the midst of our disagreements. We have human rights on account of our vulnerability to the worst excesses of power. We demand economic freedom, free markets, and private property because our life-plans are different from one another and we because we know that there is no other way to reconcile our varying preferences in a coherent way of life. And we subject ourselves to the discipline of the Rule of Law so that we can be governed in a way that respects our dignity in the forms and procedures that are used.

Each of these ideals is a response to our limits and our fallibility. And each is accompanied by misgivings about the possibility of abuse. Both the promise and the limitations of each of these ideals should be confronted explicitly and honestly without myth or fable, and a balance maintained between the demands of any one of these ideals and the demands of the others. Each of them reflects a distinct package of concerns and aspirations, and political argument probably works best when each is argued out, on its own terms, in ways that make clear the trade-offs that may be required from the other ideals. I have tried in these lectures to sustain this approach, exploring the difficulties we get into if we try to blur the distinction between (say) the Rule of Law and the ideal of economic freedom. Both are important, but it is a balance we should seek, rather than a blurring, or an assimilation, of their demands. If it is our aim to remind the common people of England of the importance of the Rule of Law, it should equally be our aim to remind them that that ideal is not the be-all and end-all and that it may have to be reconciled with other principles and ideals in the constellation of our values.

Most of all, we should not try to trick people into exaggerating the importance of any particular value or ideal by insinuating it into the fabric of our other ideals, or by using it to colonize ideals that are best stated (at least in the first instance) without reference to it. That, I fear, is what has been happening in the attempt to privilege private property and free markets under the auspices of the Rule of Law, and that has been the target of my critical remarks in these lectures. In making those critical remarks, I do not want to be read as denigrating the importance of private property, markets, and economic freedom. They are tremendously important, and no account of our political morality would be adequate if it did not give them a prominent place. They are also controversial, both in their substance and in their applications: people disagree about how much of our economy should be organized through markets, how far private property should be limited by the sort of legislative concerns we have been considering here, and how far we should establish non-market and non-property institutions to respond to the concerns about individual need unequal opportunity, and the public evils that we face. These are important controversies, and it seems to me that they are best aired and debated directly. The Rule of Law, as a political ideal, is somewhat less controversial. Maybe we should argue more about it. But, in my view, we will never get anywhere with either argument if we try to hijack the less controversial character of the one and put it to work in the controversies associated with the other.

INDEX